Children's Writing in the Primary School

UKRA Teaching of Reading Monographs

Advisory editor 1984–
Asher Cashdan, Head of Department of Communication Studies,
Sheffield City Polytechnic

Children's Writing in the Primary School
Roger Beard

Advisory editors 1977–83
Asher Cashdan
Alastair Hendry, Principal Lecturer in Primary Education,
Craigie College of Education

Listening to Children Reading
Helen Arnold

The Thoughtful Reader in the Primary School
Elizabeth Wilson

Advisory editor (1971–7)
John E. Merritt, Professor of Educational Studies,
The Open University, Milton Keynes

Reading Readiness
John Downing and Derek Thackray

Reading, Writing and Relevance
Mary Hoffman

Modern Innovations in the Teaching of Reading
Donald Moyle and Louise M. Moyle

Reading: Tests and Assessment Techniques (new edition in preparation)
Peter D. Pumfrey

Reading and the Consumer
Alma Williams

Print and Prejudice
Sarah Goodman Zimet (with an additional chapter by Mary Hoffman)

Children's Writing in the Primary School

Roger Beard

Hodder and Stoughton
In association with the United Kingdom Reading Association

British Library Cataloguing in Publication Data

Beard, Roger
   Children's writing in the primary school. – (UKRA
   teaching of reading manuscripts)
   1. Creative writing (Elementary education)
   2. English language – Study and teaching (Elementary)
   – Great Britain
   I. Title   II. Series
   372.6'23'0941   LB1576

   ISBN 0-340-35631-6

First published 1984
Copyright © 1984 Roger Beard

Printed and bound in Great Britain for
Hodder and Stoughton Educational,
a division of Hodder and Stoughton Ltd,
Mill Road, Dunton Green, Sevenoaks, Kent.
Photoset by Rowland Phototypesetting Ltd,
Bury St Edmunds, Suffolk.

Contents

Acknowledgments

A book of this kind is the culmination of years of experience and reflection and I wish to thank all those who have provided significant help over this time, including the other writers whose work I have used and who are listed at the end. In addition, I am extremely grateful to Anne Gilkes and Connie Reid for turning my untidy drafts into immaculate typescript; Pat Thomson, of the National Federation of Children's Book Groups, for our many discussions on the choice of children's books in chapter 8; Janet Wright for helping me obtain a number of less accessible publications; my wife Jenny for her continuing and patient support; Asher Cashdan, for his encouragement and fastidious editorial advice; and most of all, the teachers and children with whom I have worked in so many different ways.

Leeds, 1984   *Roger Beard*

To my daughters, Alison and Hannah

1 Why write this book?

It seems only right to begin a book on children's writing with something written by a child. In this case, hearing the opening minutes of Dylan Thomas's *Under Milk Wood* prompted Carl (9) to produce his own blank verse, headed by his own title.

Night in a country village

The silence of the nights desent is frightning
The erie hooting of the owl as he sits upon his perch
The moonlight passes over the stoops
Then the gentle breathing of the night animals suddenly ceases
The intruder is the dawn,
The badger rushes to his set and sleeps
Now over the creatures of the night there is silence
As silent as the nights desent incomes the busy ~~down~~ morn.

In many ways, this is a very mature and skilful piece of writing for a little boy of nine. But, more fundamentally, it helps us identify important questions which underlie much of what comes later in this book. What was Carl's aim in writing this? Was there something more behind his intention than just to please the teacher? Had he developed a 'sense of audience' other than the teacher in the traditional 'examiner' role? What was the basis of his choice of subject matter and its integration of first- and second-hand experience? What kind of writing is this?

These sorts of questions help bring a more professional perspective to the study of the squiggles that children make on various surfaces and which we call writing. Questions on aim, audience, content and kind, or 'mode', can be applied to virtually any writing and to the assessment of it. To acknowledge the reflexive nature of the lines which I am producing at this very moment, we can apply such questions to the making of this book, by way of introduction.

THE AIM

The aim of this book is to provide an introduction to the study of the writing done by children. Writing is one of the main features of children's primary school experiences. Recent observational studies suggest that nearly 30 per cent of junior school pupils' school time is spent in writing activities (Galton *et al.*, 1980, p. 81). Yet despite the expansion of activity in the field of language development in recent years, in publications, courses and conferences, reading has tended to receive a good deal more attention than writing. This tendency is reflected in the Bullock Report (Department of Education and Science (DES), 1975) in which five chapters are given to reading (including those on literature and reading difficulties) and only one to writing. Since then, books on the teaching of reading have considerably outnumbered those on teaching writing. Where books on the latter have been published they have tended to be related to the secondary school age range (e.g. Burgess *et al.*, 1973; Britton *et al.*, 1975; Martin *et al.*, 1976). Books for teachers of younger children have tended to adopt a narrow theoretical perspective, such as 'creative writing' (Lane and Kemp, 1967; Maybury, 1967; Marshall, 1974). Some have not made their theoretical perspective explicit (Armitstead, 1972), while others have widened their framework but failed to treat it critically (e.g. Rosen and Rosen, 1973; Hutchcroft *et al.*, 1981).

The most wide-ranging and substantial book on younger children's writing is that of Harpin (1976) which looks at a whole range of issues. Yet here, too, there are limitations: the book concentrates on the junior school years and only sketches out a few principles for classroom work with children. Furthermore, recent research findings have become available in, for example, the surveys of English primary schools and first schools by Her Majesty's Inspectorate (HMI) (DES, 1978; 1982a), the detailed studies of junior school life by the University of Leicester ORACLE project (Galton *et al.*, 1980), and the Schools Council report on Open Plan primary schools (Bennett *et al.*, 1980). Sources such as these offer indications of broad patterns of classroom practice which can help highlight 'structural' weaknesses and strengths; they also offer a helpful basis for comparison with the trends and practices in any school or classroom. In these ways, the studies provide an incentive for teachers to adopt the ancient Greek slogan 'Know thyself' and to consider the implications for professional development which stem from this kind of self-evaluation.

At the same time, important research studies have been going on in the United States, Canada and the United Kingdom into the nature of the writing process and its development in children (e.g. Graves, 1975; Bereiter, 1980; Kroll *et al.*, 1980). Therefore the making of a new book on children's writing allows its readers to weigh up recent developments in the study of written language from a variety of theoretical perspectives, and to consider some practical implications. Nevertheless, before firm decisions can be taken about the details of what such a book might contain, thoughts have to be given to the second aspect, the audience for whom the book is intended.

THE AUDIENCE

The main audience for this book is clearly those who teach in primary or middle schools, or those being trained to do so. Taking the larger of these groups first, qualified teachers may come across this book in a variety of ways, browsing in a bookshop, library or at a conference book-stall; having it 'set' on an in-service course; taking it down from a staffroom bookshelf in a search for inspiration or how to plan for the following week or the following term, or, at a push, the following lesson! Each of these possibilities assumes certain audience needs. The browsing teacher may be looking for a book to use or dip into for a variety of reasons in the weeks ahead: for reviewing ideas on developing writing which have evolved since he or she was trained; for ideas and sources to improve children's spelling; to look for a framework which confirms his or her best practices but which may also help identify the weaknesses, perhaps part of the evolution of a school-focused language policy.

The teacher on the in-service course, be it a short course, BEd, Diploma, MA or MEd, will be looking for more than this. A rigorous analysis of competing ideas in the field of language studies may be wanted: 'What exactly did Britton say?' 'How do his ideas relate to those of Bereiter?' For such teachers references to the most significant publications and a bibliography will be invaluable for essays, special studies and theses.

The teacher who is looking for practical suggestions for forthcoming lessons represents another range of audience needs. Specific topics, perhaps related to a coherent curriculum network of some kind; some indications of promising patterns of classroom organisation; rich sources of prose and poetry to read to and discuss with the children – all may figure in this teacher's consciousness.

While the needs of each of these kinds of teacher audience have to be kept in mind, those of other kinds of audience have to be anticipated too. Student teachers' needs will be similar except that their perspective will be a more prospective one. With little previous experience of work with children to draw upon, they will be looking for a book which tries to introduce the range of options open to them. Such an inductive approach can help them avoid the relative neglect of some aspects of writing, such as letter formation with younger children or the encouragement of the writing of extended arguments with older ones. Teachers in training will need these considerations to be set against other broader ones related to overall writing development within the school curriculum context.

Generally speaking, writers of books for pre-service teacher training tend to adopt one of two contrasting approaches, 'instructional' or 'professional'. The temptation to take an 'instructional' approach, which uncritically presents a range of practical ideas, is understandable, given the perennial criticisms on the education and training of teachers. At the same time, the dangers of indoctrination have to be faced. Unless it is clear that the practical ideas put forward will have optimum effectiveness under any circumstances, the status of such ideas can be only provisional.

An important alternative to the uncritical instructional approach is the kind of 'professional' perspective exemplified by Smith's (1978a, 1978b) books on reading. Smith argues that in place of advice on instruction, teachers should be introduced to information on the nature of the reading process, so that they can then make up their own minds on teaching approaches in the most reliable, professional way. The key, then, is understanding the process, a suggestion which is equally applicable to writing as Smith (1982) has recently shown.

> Without such understanding, teachers cannot make up their own minds about methods and materials, and are forced to fall back on the exhortations of experts or the importunings of publishers. Such teachers must work without knowing why they succeed or fail. Without understanding, instruction is founded on superstition (Smith, 1978b, pp. 4–5).

Smith's views may be given an additional significance when set against the recent growth of demands for greater teacher accountability. As Sockett (1976) has pointed out, such demands may be better met by building accountability into a 'professional' rather than an 'utilitarian' model of teaching. A professional model of accountability would ensure that priority would be given to principles of practice, rather than results of performance; accountability would be to a variety of people, agencies and institutions, rather than 'the public' alone; and the teacher would be seen as an autonomous professional rather than a social technician. This kind of argument links neatly with those of Smith. An 'established professional view' of the development of children's writing could act as a basic frame of reference for use in appraising the needs of particular schools and children. Difficulties may lie in the agreement of this established view, but the broad direction of the professional model of accountability and teacher education seems more promising for teachers as a whole.

Even so, making insights into language processes available to student teachers and then encouraging them to make their own decisions on teaching approaches may seem unnecessarily indirect. Smith's viewpoint could well be connected with the fact that his career of naval officer, journalist and academic has not included school teaching. Writers of books for use in initial teacher training who can combine relevant teaching experience with the products of serious academic study may well add a further insight to the professional perspective on teacher training. In particular, they can give some indications of the main practical implications which stem from different notions of the writing process.

Two other kinds of audience need also to be borne in mind. Academic colleagues in colleges, polytechnics and universities, whose work includes helping students and teachers to understand and develop children's writing, should find that this book can be of value. Although it is obviously not written specifically for them, it has been prepared with an eye cast in their direction. Each would have his or her own priorities on preparing a book of this kind. Many will have the benefit of lengthy experience of teaching, school visits, courses and conferences, as well as the continuing support of an academic community served by a specialised library. Their response to a new book on children's writing will inevitably involve a scholarly appraisal of it. Thus in setting out to write this book I am obviously aware that they '. . . are there, mostly friendly but untrue to their calling if not also critical' (Halsey, 1981, p. vi).

Parents may form the smallest of the audiences, but they too will have particular needs when consulting a book on children's writing. These needs may include seeking background information on how children's writing develops and how it may be fostered, to inform themselves on current thinking in the educational world on the kinds of writing the children can undertake, to increase their awareness of what problems children may experience in writing and what children are capable of as they increase their confidence and as their abilities mature through the primary and middle school years.

To attempt to bear these overlapping yet distinctive audiences in mind is a major undertaking, but the aim of this book is sharpened in attempting to do exactly this. The means by which these varying audience needs can be met will be at least partly specified by considering the content with particular care.

THE CONTENT

What goes into a book of this kind is inevitably the result of an extremely complex series of selections from the fields of knowledge which seem to offer most assistance to anyone concerned with fostering children's writing. Many fields might be identified in this way. In the context of compiling the present book, those which seemed to offer most were psychology, linguistics and the teaching of English.

Psychology offers us insights into how children learn, what motivates them and the possible origins of their learning difficulties. The nature of the insights will vary according to which area of psychology is consulted. One recent estimate is that there are 75 distinct areas within the subject (Giorgi, 1976). The potential contribution to our understanding of children's writing has been enhanced in recent years by a trend within psychology which can be called 'humanistic'. A notable feature of this trend is that increasing numbers of studies are prepared to take into account the meanings which individuals attach to their actions and situations, rather than treating them in a purely objective way in monitoring their behaviour.

A particularly relevant kind of study which exemplifies this trend is Margaret Donaldson's (1978) *Children's Minds*. She points out that as children are introduced to written language,

> . . . many of them will never before have realised that the flow of speech, which they have been producing and interpreting unreflectingly for years, is composed of *words*. Yet this realisation is indispensable if they are to deal sensibly with the grouped and spaced marks on paper which, as they must now come to see, correspond to the spoken language . . . (p. 97).

Donaldson stresses the importance of teachers being able to extend their sense of empathy and to 'decentre', by placing themselves imaginatively in the child's position in the general experience of school life.

In some ways, this sensitivity to the pupil's perspective resembles the phenomenological perspective in the sociology of education, which stresses individuals' subjective understanding. Typical of this perspective is the celebrated essay by Alfred Schutz called 'The Stranger' (Cosin *et al.*, 1971), in which the problems of an individual adjusting to the patterns of behaviour and expectations of an institution are explored, problems which can often be paralleled in the uncertainties experienced by children on entering school.

From the 'how' of learning, we can turn to the 'what'. Linguistics can provide insights into the nature of language, its variety and development. Despite an enormous growth in interest in this field in the past two decades or so, many of those working with children still may not fully appreciate how much of our experience of the world and especially of schools is mediated through language. The structure of our spoken language, made up of a system of sounds, meanings and grammatical rules, provides an inescapable 'filter' through which much of our reality is processed.

Children's writing evolves from the use of this structure and related teaching and learning processes are inevitably bound up with it. Any decisions in the classroom on the setting or marking of children's writing, or on ways of improving spelling, for example, will inevitably carry with them assumptions on the nature of this structure and the ways in which it may mature. Such assumptions will need to be critically assessed and perhaps modified if teaching opportunities are to be maximised.

The teaching of English can offer perspectives on the ways in which the processes of learning how to use language can be best fostered. It has been characterised by controversies within itself in recent years and these add to the complexity of making a selection from it. Although the controversies have been centred on the secondary age-range, it is easy to see how they carry over into the issues surrounding teaching in the primary years. Dixon (1975) draws a generalised but useful distinction between three models of English teaching based on skills, personal growth and cultural heritage. Although aspects of all three can be found in primary school teaching, it is the first which probably dominates.

The HMI primary school survey (DES, 1978, p. 51) reports that: 'Text books containing comprehension, grammar and language exercises ... featured in the work of almost every nine- and eleven-year-old class, and of about two-thirds of seven-year-old classes.' In contrast, writing on subjects of children's own choice not necessarily connected with other current school work was seen in only just over half the classes observed. If this is taken as a provisional index of the development of a 'personal growth' model, the suggestion here is that the skills of 'language study' through exercises are given more attention than the 'language use' (Britton, 1971) of personal writing and responses to literature, for example.

Tentative though this suggestion is, any relation to the 'cultural heritage' model must be even more cautious, partly because it tends to be more easily identifiable in the English subject teaching of secondary and tertiary education and partly because it is difficult to find any kind of gross index of its adoption. Certainly it seems that children have stories read to them in most junior school classes (DES, 1978, p. 50). Yet in what evidence there is of children's reading interests in the middle years, 'quality' authors are scarcely featured (Whitehead, 1977). Whatever reservations there might be about notions of quality, there is supporting evidence of a more recent kind (Bird, 1982) that direct use of the so-called 'golden age' of children's literature (Ellis, 1968) is not so widespread in the primary and middle curriculum as might be expected.

Overall, then, it seems that there may be considerable untapped potential for exploiting the latter two of the models from the teaching of English which Dixon puts forward, personal growth and cultural heritage, to help enrich the context of children writing in the five to 13 age-range, as well as providing more substantial resources for the exercises which seem to be so widely practised.

To these possibilities for enrichment and the insights from psychology and linguistics can be added one more perspective, the professional and personal judgement of myself as a writer. The selection from the above fields is essentially a personal one, influenced by the experiences of teaching in primary schools, lecturing in a college of higher education, visiting dozens of schools and working with numerous in-service education groups. The stamp of personal experience is given a greater intensity in the many extracts of children's writing. Nearly all are drawn from my own teaching experience.

THE MODE

The notion of the 'mode' of a piece of writing fits rather uneasily into this context. Alternative terms like 'kind', 'category' or 'genre' might be used instead to distinguish between descriptions, narratives or evaluations. Such alternatives carry with them ambiguities which perhaps mode does not, and therefore the latter is preferred. By using 'mode' in this way, attention can be drawn to what in other circles might be called the 'genre' of the writing in this book: an evaluation of some of the principal issues in a particular area of education, and the suggestion of some tentative implications for classroom practice.

A central feature of this evaluation will be a discussion of the ways in which aims of writing can be classified. In such a discussion, some important dilemmas which face teachers can be examined. These dilemmas centre on the basic decision as to what kinds of writing to seek to develop in children. For some teachers, the decision may be expressed in the question: 'What replaces "the composition"?' Others may ask, 'Creative writing and what else?' Indications of lack of agreement about different aims of writing have come from in-service courses I have run, in which teachers have been asked to produce some writing and ascribe a label to it. Such an activity can generate a range of terms like personal, creative, informative, and narrative. If teacher education is going to develop its work on writing in ways which are comparable to those associated with reading, it seems likely that greater awareness and agreement will need to evolve in the profession on how these sorts of labels relate to each other. The Bullock Report adopted the function categories of James Britton (DES, 1975, ch. 11), but since then certain aspects of this model have been fiercely criticised. Some of the features of these criticisms and Britton's reply will be dealt with later. For the moment, it is important to establish that these uncertainties about different writing aims do exist. Such uncertainties will be part of the individual store of ideas which all teachers will have, however dubious they are about educational 'theory'. As Lawton (1974, p. 37) has pointed out:

> Although many teachers object to discussions about theory in education, in fact all teachers operate with some kind of theoretical framework at the back of their minds . . . Every time a teacher in the staffroom suggests that a certain textbook is too difficult for a class or a group he is making assumptions about the nature of ability and child development – assumptions of a highly theoretical nature.

This is not to suggest that a single model of writing 'aims' will ever dominate educational thought or that it is desirable that it should. Yet there are strong arguments for suggesting that the education of many children would be enriched if there was a consensus reached on these matters, at least among teachers who work together. Such discussions would be best held together in some form of policy or guidelines which tend to evolve in the kinds of school-focused INSET activities which have increased in recent years (Henderson, 1979; Donoughue et al., 1981). Recommendations for use in such policy development are given in chapter 10.

WRITING AND LANGUAGE AND LEARNING

These and other considerations can be taken up later, but for the moment the basic points of this introductory chapter can be summarised. Any act of writing will normally involve the basic 'parameters' of aim, audience, content and mode. To make the most of opportunities for improving the quality and effectiveness of children's writing, these parameters and their inter-relationships will demand continuing scrutiny. It is also important to establish two further considerations of fundamental significance. One is that any writing is only part of the complex web of language skills which also includes talking, listening and reading. Opportunities for learning are likely to be fulfilled only when the potential of each of these in any task is properly utilised. What is more, any attempts to assess and develop children's skills in writing need to be continually related to the potential use of these other language skills. Secondly, writing in school will take place within the broad context of the curriculum, its aims, teaching approaches, content and evaluation. As a former Chief Inspector of Primary Schools has pointed out, within this context children will develop knowledge, ideas, skills and attitudes (Thomas, 1980). This book, therefore, attempts to set the development of children's writing within a perspective which includes some consideration of broader language and curriculum issues.

Chapter 3 examines the nature of the writing process, in relation to the forms and functions of language in general. Chapter 4 summarises some of the most significant research studies on several different dimensions by which children's writing develops over time.

Chapter 5 reviews the different categories of writing types adopted in various post-war publications. Also in this chapter a coherent framework of different writing aims is set out and this is used as a basis for later discussion of a range of examples of children's writing.

The early stages of writing are considered in chapter 6 and chapter 7 begins with some reference to the curriculum context within which writing in schools is done. The rest of chapter 7 and chapter 8 contain a discussion of children's writing, within the particular theoretical framework established earlier. Chapter 9 suggests some possible ways of assessing children's writing and helping them improve it. The final chapter draws a number of issues together in a set of recommendations for use in school language policies.

To begin with, however, it will be useful to examine in the next chapter the evidence of the writing which goes on in primary schools, so that this book can be read with the most significant findings in mind.

2 Observations of children writing

Before examining the nature of the writing process and how it can be developed in children, it is important to look at recent research into what goes on in schools in the primary age-range. In recent years a considerable amount of information has been collected on this, much of it by discreet observational research methods. This chapter looks at the accumulated evidence on the time spent by children writing, how this relates to general patterns of classroom activity and considers some possible implications.

SOURCES OF OBSERVATIONAL RESEARCH

Two reports by Her Majesty's Inspectorate (HMI) (DES, 1978, 1982a) have given an indication of activities in 542 primary schools (where only junior classes were observed) and 80 first schools respectively during the inspectors' visits. Inevitably, cautions have to be borne in mind about the representativeness of the sampled schools and classes and the effect of the presence of HMI in the classroom, but the reports are an important source of knowledge on the work of schools. Many teachers will agree that a short time visiting another school provides many helpful possibilities for making a cool, detached appraisal of the nature and distribution of pupils' activities through a school day, and this is the kind of information which the two HMI reports convey and relate to general trends.

The research reports by the ORACLE team at the University of Leicester (Galton *et al.*, 1980) provide a different kind of data. This 'Observational Research And Classroom Learning Evaluation' project has attempted to provide a reasonably objective data base on the kinds of teaching and learning activities which are evidenced in today's schools. ORACLE's first study involved carrying out systematic observations in 58 primary classrooms from three local education authorities (LEAs) on a time-sampled basis, as part of a longitudinal study of activity, progress and performance.

The survey by Bennett *et al.* (1980) of patterns of organisation in twenty-three junior and infant open plan schools also used observation schedules as part of a larger study of such schools in 18 local education authorities. The sample was selected to examine practices in open plan schools with different arrangements of classroom 'units' and therefore should not be seen as necessarily representative of schools of more traditional design. The schedules of observations in this research involved logging the activities of pupils of different abilities within units, at intervals throughout the school day (excluding breaks) for several days.

Incidental information on pupils' experience of writing in school has also come from two other research projects funded by the Schools Council which have been primarily concerned with reading (Lunzer and Gardner, 1979; Southgate *et al.*, 1981). Lunzer and Gardner's studies of average and above average readers in the ten to 15 age-range included observational research using a Reading Behaviour Inventory on which the activities of 'target' pupils could be noted (Dolan *et al.*, 1979). The inventory was designed specifically to monitor the incidence and context of reading, but other activities were checked as well. Nine primary schools from two local education authorities were included for the research, selected because they were 'feeder' schools to the secondary schools on which the research was centred. The total observation time in primary schools was nearly 50 hours in English, mathematics, science and social studies lessons.

The report by Southgate *et al.* (1981) provides some detailed information on the writing tasks undertaken in 33 first and second year junior classes in twelve schools. These schools from four local education authorities in the North of England were studied intensively in the second stage of an investigation into extending beginning reading.

Taken together, these different reports provide some glimpses of patterns of work in schools, from which a few tentative conclusions can be drawn about the writing which is going on. However imperfect the relationship between these studies, an examination of their findings can provide both useful pointers for future research and some general yardsticks against which any teachers can assess the circumstances under which their own pupils write.

TIME ON TASK

In terms of quantitative results, these various studies suggest that, perhaps not surprisingly, children are generally involved in writing tasks for considerable proportions of the school day, every day. The ORACLE study reports that junior school children spend about a third of the day on writing concerned with 'language' tasks and a further quarter on 'general studies' (history, geography, science, religious studies, including 'topic work'), let alone the writing involved in mathematics, which takes up a further third of curriculum time.

The research study by Bennett *et al.* (1980) tends to confirm that a great deal of writing is going on in schools. Infants were observed as being allocated opportunities for language work (in which writing seemed to play a large part) for an average of 36 per cent of their time in their open plan classrooms, although the range between classroom units was from 28 per cent to 48 per cent. In junior classrooms 'language' was given less time: on average, 31 per cent, although the range was greater, 17–46 per cent. This large range is partly explained by the fact that some schools devoted much more time to 'environmental studies' than others.

In the area of Lunzer and Gardner's (1979) research projects which dealt with the incidence and context of various language activities in the classroom, a rather different finding appears. In top junior classes, the percentage of time spent writing by observed pupils was only 15 per cent of lessons, ranging from 5 per cent in mathematics (although another quarter of the lessons were spent in 'calculating') to 22 per cent in science (Dolan *et al.*, 1979). At first this may seem rather less than might be expected after examining the findings reported by Galton *et al.* and Bennett *et al.* However, in Dolan's study, only the time in which a pupil was physically putting pen (or pencil) to paper was coded as 'writing'. This raises the issue of the proportion of time pupils spend in planning what they are going to write or indeed engaging in activities not at all related to school work. Dolan *et al.* report that the average amount of 'deliberation' in writing tasks was in fact low, only 4 per cent, with a small range. Average non-involvement in the lesson was higher, 12 per cent, and the maximum tended to be in English (16 per cent).

Southgate *et al.* found a much higher incidence of 'non-involvement' in observations of the seven to nine age-range and discusses this finding in detail. Between first and second year junior classes there appeared to be a considerable switch in emphasis of writing tasks in the observed classes, from 20 per cent writing without the aid of books and 7 per cent writing referring to books in the first year to an almost exact reversal of these proportions in the second year. This striking shift of emphasis is explained by the great increase in 'topic work' in second year junior classes and an increase in the amount of time spent on comprehension exercises.

While the 'deliberating' time was perhaps a little higher than that reported by Dolan *et al.* from top junior classes, 'non-involvement' was much higher, being observed as 33 per cent of the pupils' lesson time in both age-ranges. The figure needs to be related to an enormous range of 0 per cent to 88 per cent non-involvement, and large fluctuations within individual pupil behaviour, according to apparent motivation and organisational changes.

The issue of non-involvement in set tasks is also taken up by Galton *et al.* and by Bennett *et al.* The latter note that in infant classroom units 16 per cent of the total school day (including administration/transition time but excluding breaks) of the sampled pupils could be classified as 'non-involvement'. Especially in language activities, the average non-involvement was 22 per cent, ranging from 10 per cent to 36 per cent. In junior classroom units, non-involvement was near 21 per cent of the total school day on average but generally higher in language, where it averaged 30 per cent, ranging from 15 per cent to 50 per cent.

Galton *et al.* take the study of non-involvement and although they do not relate it to curriculum areas, they do put forward some 'pupil types' to describe recurring differences between individual patterns of behaviour. On the basis of the ORACLE findings in junior classrooms, a 'typical' pupil concentrates on 'the job in hand' for three-fifths of the time, although this figure rises to three-quarters when other 'routine' tasks are taken into consideration, such as waiting for the teacher to check work. Of the resulting figure of 25 per cent total non-involvement, over half comprises being distracted in some way, but it includes very little horseplay (0.2 per cent).

PUPIL TYPES

It is important to add that Galton *et al.* then go on to identify four main types of pupil behaviour and reference to these will give some idea of the variations found. Just under a third of the pupils in the sample were seen as 'intermittent workers', being involved with set tasks or associated routines 64 per cent of the time and having the lowest interaction with the teacher but the highest with other pupils, 'flitting from one brief conversation to another' in between getting on with the task. Just under a third of the pupils were classified as 'solitary workers', having low levels of interaction with teacher or pupils, but being involved in tasks or routines more than any other group (77 per cent of the time). Nearly a fifth of the pupils were termed 'attention seekers', being involved in tasks or routines for two-thirds of the time, but having the highest levels of interaction with the teacher, much of which is initiated by the pupils themselves and is concerned with routine or task work.

The smallest group to be identified were the 'quiet collaborators', 12 per cent of the sample, who had the second highest work rate after the solitary workers but whose interaction levels with the teacher were higher than the latter. Galton provides a similar analysis of teacher types and begins to relate the way in which the pupil/teacher types interact and influence academic performance. His findings are referred to again in chapter 7 in a discussion of some of the main issues of curriculum and classroom organisation related to children's writing.

Before considering the general implications of these various quantitative findings, some of the evidence on qualitative aspects of writing needs to be mentioned and such evidence largely comes from the two DES surveys of primary schools (concentrating on the seven to 11 age-range) and of first schools (concentrating on the five to eight or five to nine age-range).

TYPES OF TASK

If we look at the overall context of writing in the primary years of schooling, there are strong suggestions in the HMI reports that writing activities are sometimes too bound to copying from cards and completing exercises from work cards and textbooks. It is suggested in the first school report that, in the early stages of writing, copying activities should be more related to children's own words and sentences, rather than those arbitrarily selected.

In some schools the tendency for writing to be particularly caught up with copying from cards and books was even more noticeable in the older children's work. The primary survey reports that 'topic work' consisted of copying from reference books in two-thirds of nine-year-old classes and four-fifths of 11-year-old classes, a proportion deemed 'excessive' by HMI. Furthermore, copying from the blackboard took 'too prominent a place' in about a third of the classes in the nine and 11-year-old age-ranges. This concern is similar to that expressed by the Bullock Committee: 'the experience of our visits was that much of the writing done in the name of topic work amounts to no more than copying' (DES, 1975, p. 393).

Another general aspect of the context of children writing in school is its point of departure. Children did some writing on subjects of their own choice unconnected with school work in just over half the classes in the primary survey, and related to school work in just under half. It was more common for teachers to set the writing tasks themselves.

In examining the attention given to the 'forms' of children's writing, the findings on handwriting seem a little inconsistent. The primary school survey suggests that practice in developing this skill was being given in nearly all seven to 11 classes sampled, whereas in the first school survey the five to nine schools especially seemed to neglect this provision on a systematic basis. Only a minority of schools ensured regular practice in letter formation and provided opportunities for children to take pride in producing pieces of handwriting of an aesthetically pleasing quality.

In the case of another major aspect of 'form', spelling, the findings are more consistent. The primary school survey suggests that spelling was being taught through the use of textbooks in the majority of seven-year-old classes and nearly all the classes of older pupils. The first school survey confirms this tendency to give regular attention to spelling in the five to eight or nine age-ranges. Here word lists, dictation, copying and correcting of errors, and particularly learning lists of words for homework, seemed widespread. The authors of the report add that frequently this work was inefficiently planned in that the children knew many of the words in the first place, or were being given many new words that they were unlikely to use in the normal context of their school work.

THE AIMS OF CHILDREN'S WRITING

What kinds of writing tasks were being undertaken in the surveyed schools? Evidence from the studies reviewed here does not provide very much substantial information to help answer this question, but there are some general tendencies which can be identified. To sketch an answer, the simple framework outlined in the previous chapter will be used: aims, audience, content and mode. Aims will be dealt with first, using the framework for analysing the aims of writing adopted in this book from Kinneavy's (1971) work, expressive, literary, referential (or expository) and persuasive (see chapters 5, 7 and 8). In what is reported by the HMI surveys, personal, 'expressive' writing featured increasingly by age-range in primary classrooms and was encouraged in first schools although the inspectors suggest that more of it would benefit children, in particular where over-use of exercises and work cards seriously curtails the time available for continuous writing.

There also seemed to be much writing of a 'literary' kind, notably in the form of stories being written by children which were to be found in nearly all the classes in the primary survey. So-called 'creative writing' where children are 'primed' into producing 'colourful or fanciful language . . . using vivid imagery' (DES, 1975, p. 163) was not found as often as the inspectors had anticipated, confirming the ORACLE finding in which it occupied 8 per cent of the available curriculum time as against 25 per cent on other 'language' activities. The authors of the primary survey express relief at this finding, in that creative writing can often be 'divorced from real feeling', whereas the first school survey expresses some regret that more poetry was not being written by children in the five to nine age-range.

In the general area of 'expository' writing first schools appeared to be more varied in their provision of opportunities, with HMI reporting a reasonable standard of recording, leading on to a concentration in some schools on factual writing, as in science or more functional tasks like recipes. In contrast, as was mentioned earlier, the primary survey notes the predominance of copying from reference books in relation to the kind of writing concerned with expository aims.

There appeared to be little attention given to what can be called 'persuasive writing' in the results of either survey. While this is perhaps to be expected in the first schools because of the relatively difficult nature of the task, the primary survey suggests that, with older and more able pupils, perhaps more encouragement could be given to helping children to present a coherent argument, explore alternative possibilities, or draw conclusions and make judgements, which all can be integral parts of persuasion. The first school survey adds that children were rarely introduced to new syntactic structures, such as those of purpose or cause and effect, which seem likely to be an important part of fostering children's skills in developing written arguments.

THE AUDIENCE FOR CHILDREN'S WRITING

Evidence about the audience for the writing reported from first and primary schools is even more elusive, and again inferences have to be very tentative. It seems reasonable to assume that in some ways much of the writing was done to try to 'please the teacher' in a narrow sense. The first school survey, while noting teachers' lack of success in 'the difficult goal of giving real inspiration', records that 'teachers gave a good deal of praise and encouragement', presumably in the light of how the writing related to their own criteria for assessing the writing performance of young children. The survey report goes on to hint that one of the teachers' main priorities was 'the introduction of new words'. At the same time, the primary survey suggests that the majority of teachers in the seven to 11 age-range were not using children's written work in a diagnostic way to help develop appropriate teaching of spelling, syntax, structure or style. The primary survey reports that children were actively encouraged to share with other pupils what they had written in just under half the classes. This was done by means of classroom books, magazines, plays, real letters or occasionally in corresponding with another school.

THE CONTENT OF CHILDREN'S WRITING

The evidence on the content of children's writing shows little indication of any particular pattern, other than in the youngest age-ranges. Here it was common for 'news' pictures to be drawn by the children, with the teachers adding captions which the children then traced or copied. From here, the generalisations and examples in the first school survey suggest that the tendency for content to be related to personal experience was maintained both in diaries, letters and newspapers, and also in factual writing related to the curriculum. Many schools seemed also to encourage children to base their writing on more imaginative content, probably through the writing and retelling of stories, of which there was 'a good deal'. The use of topics, such as 'air' or 'transport', provided content for children's writing as well as more imaginative themes in which music or visual material might be used to provide support. However, it was felt that in many schools appropriate use of a range and variety of content was not being allowed to develop in the seven to nine age-range because of an 'excessive and purposeless' use of English exercises from commercially-produced books and cards. Even teacher-made cards designed as 'stimuli' sometimes resulted in rather stereotyped writing from children.

The primary school survey reports that in the seven to 11 age-range these trends are continued, with content for writing often being related to personal experiences outside school, school-based visits, or the school surroundings. With seven-year-olds, imaginative or constructive play was used as a basis for language activities which included writing in nearly two-thirds of the classes. Books of exercises were used in the majority of seven-year-old classes and virtually all the classes of nine- and 11-year-olds. Again, the report points out that isolated exercises do not necessarily help children to write 'fluently and with purpose'.

There is little evidence from the other research studies on the content of children's writing, although Southgate et al. (1981, p. 149) hint that writing tasks which demanded that they used their imaginations seemed beyond some children observed by the researchers in first and second year junior classes.

MODES OF CHILDREN'S WRITING

Finally, the reports give some information on the different modes of children's writing. The primary school survey reports that narrative writing was found in virtually all the sampled classes. This writing was related both to the real world and imaginative experiences, and sometimes included children describing their own experiences. The report sets this against 'creative writing', defined as prose or poetry which is 'expressive of feeling', and says that this was not being encouraged in schools as much as had been expected. 'Personal writing recreating experiences faithfully and sincerely' was much more frequent although more evaluative writing (presenting arguments, exploring possibilities, making judgements) was rarely found, even with older or more able pupils.

The first school survey seems to use a different kind of framework, distinguishing between stories, factual recording and descriptive writing, all of which emerged in the five- to six-year-old age-range. In the section on 'different kinds of writing', there is also mention of personal writing and imaginative writing, with the additional note that little writing of poetry was seen.

The ORACLE study classifies language work into reading, writing, spoken English and creative writing without specifically defining what the latter involves. The category 'general studies' includes the writing tasks involved in a number of curriculum areas, including topic work, although no particular kind of writing is noted.

Bennett *et al.* used the categories of free writing and comprehension writing as well as handwriting and copy writing in their observation schedules. Southgate *et al.* also use the term 'free writing' and appear to use it synonymously with 'creative writing'. Together, the two are contrasted with 'writing with the aid of reference materials, such as information books or word cards'.

IMPLICATIONS OF OBSERVATIONAL RESEARCH ON CHILDREN'S WRITING

One not unexpected general finding from these reports is that substantial amounts of the school day are given over to writing, often more than any other activity. The finding on children's 'non-involvement' with school tasks is probably less expected. Many teachers might be rather surprised at the proportions of the children in these studies who appear to be working the equivalent of a four-day week. But the implications of these findings are more complex than at first might appear.

The relationship between children's perception of school tasks, the balance of time spent on them and other circumstances is clearly a complex one. Although factors like teaching style and the intrinsic interest of the subject-matter will have some influence, another central issue is what children see themselves as doing when they are putting pen or pencil to paper. Their awareness of what they are trying to do may well be closely related to their involvement in it. Certainly the non-involvement noted by Southgate *et al.* varied enormously, between o per cent and 88 per cent, indicating how much children will adapt to circumstances. It must also be noted that, according to Bennett *et al.*, non-involvement tended to be higher in the writing tasks in 'language' than almost any other curriculum area. It would be helpful to assess how far non-involvement in writing tasks can be lessened if teachers and pupils together give more explicit attention to some of the key 'parameters' of writing such as aim, audience, content and mode.

Again, though, there must be a caution. Involvement is not always easy to gauge from observational data. The research by Dolan *et al.* only noted pen-to-paper time anyway, but the observers in the other surveys generally tried to infer 'involvement' from what they saw from a distance. Yet this kind of inference is not always easy to make reliably. Preparation for writing may be idiosyncratic and even professional writers plan and compose in ways which have apparently little to do with physically putting marks on paper. In general, there are strong pointers towards the need for developing classroom research in ways which can attempt to monitor the overall process of the writing being done, including such 'components' as planning and reviewing.

Coupled with this is the related need to develop a greater professional understanding of what is involved in writing. The development of such activities as planning, composing and reviewing in children deserve considerably more attention because the extent of teachers' common awareness of the nature of the writing process may well be very limited. Much of the research and many of the publications currently available are focused on the products of children's writing. Not only will greater attention on process be a more realistic focus, but it should also provide a surer foundation for assessment, marking and the diagnosis of weaknesses.

A third implication of these studies is that more attention might generally be given to the language used to describe the kinds of writing undertaken by children. Other than the almost ubiquitous use of the term 'creative writing', there is relatively little agreement within these reports on the verbal labels attached to the different writing tasks which they describe and comment upon. As will be shown later, such a lack of agreement is common to many other publications. Moreover, the labels which are used do not always make it clear whether they relate to the 'aim' of writing or the 'mode' of writing as it appears on the page. The different labels and the problems they can pose will be dealt with in chapter 5.

Finally, the reports suggest that the teaching of some of the component skills of writing is patchy. The teaching of spelling, for example, seems to be systematically undertaken in some schools and neglected by others. This represents an uneven response to the recommendation of the Bullock Committee that 'spelling needs to be taught according to a carefully worked out policy' (DES, 1975, p.528). Handwriting similarly seems to receive uneven attention. This suggests that there is considerable room for a re-examination of the time provided for the development of the skills demanded in writing. The HMI surveys, like the Bullock Report, are generally critical of the widespread use of traditional 'English exercises' for developing children's writing. It seems likely that much of the time taken up by these could be profitably channelled into more sensitive teaching of skills such as planning, reviewing, handwriting and spelling in relation to both the curriculum of the school and the abilities and needs of the children in the class. Some detailed suggestions for such teaching are given later in the book (especially in chapter 9).

For teaching of this kind to be realistically conceived, it will need to take account of the overall process of writing and its various components. The nature of this process is introduced and discussed in the next chapter.

3 The writing process and its components

Books on reading have sometimes been criticised for treating their subject too narrowly. It has been suggested that they have neglected the nature and functions of other forms of language, especially spoken language, which is normally well developed in children before they learn to read. Similarly, it is all too easy for a book on writing to be too narrowly based. It may be useful, therefore, to offer in this chapter a brief summary of the principal forms and functions of spoken language and to establish the key differences between talking and writing before examining the nature of the writing process in detail.

Writing is one of the four modes of the system of human communication that we call language. It is a capacity which, together with talking, listening and reading, sets people clearly apart from other creatures of the earth on the evolutionary scale.

Even creatures as small as bees can communicate with each other on, for example, the nature, direction and distance of a food source. They do this by 'dancing' in ways instinctively 'programmed' for them by their nervous system. Not surprisingly the far more complex nervous systems of humans allow a far greater range of communication, not so much through the number of communication units available, such as sounds and words, but because of the quality of human language often called 'open-endedness'. This quality allows the finite 'means' of sounds and words to be used in infinite permutations to produce an apparently limitless range of 'ends' in the meanings created.

LANGUAGE AND ITS FUNCTIONS

Moreover, human language is essentially a symbolic system of communication by which the world is 'represented'. It is true, of course, that human beings can also represent the world in other ways, particularly by actions or images. Children come to understand how to tie shoe laces by actually tying them; when using construction toys, they will be guided by the illustrations. It is language, though, which provides the most flexible means of representing the world, at first by speech and later by writing. This symbolic system is used in arbitrary ways to represent the world, according to culture or nationality. More importantly, the symbols can be continually reordered to create representations of past, present and future. As the Bullock Report (DES, 1975, p. 47) recognises:

... what makes us typically human is the fact that we symbolise, or represent to ourselves, the objects, people and events that make up our environment, and do so cumulatively, thus creating an inner representation of the world as we have encountered it. The accumulated representation is on the one hand a storehouse of past experience and on the other a body of expectations regarding what may yet happen to us. In this way we construct for ourselves a past and a future, a retrospect and a prospect; all our significant actions are performed within this extended field or framework ...

Psychologists have disagreed on how central language is to thinking abilities. Luria (1959), for example, sees language as central to cognitive growth; for Piaget (1959) activity and experience are more important. Similarly, linguists differ on the network of functions they attribute to language. For Halliday (1970) there are three: the 'ideational' function, in which language helps give structure to experience; the 'interpersonal', establishing and maintaining social relations; and the 'textual' function in which language is used for making links with itself and with the situation.

In her research into young children's uses of spoken language, Tough (1977) found Halliday's categories to be too broad for distinguishing between the kinds of meanings which could be communicated. Tough therefore devised a different framework for the classification of children's uses of language. Her four main functions of language (directive, interpretative, projective and relational) are in turn sub-divided into uses and strategies. For example, the directive function has two main uses, self-directing and other-directing, and the latter has four strategies, demonstrating, instructing, forward planning and anticipating collaborative action.

Not surprisingly such an ambitious scheme has brought its criticisms. Wells (1977), for instance, reports his difficulty in trying to apply Tough's categories to utterances such as 'I'm wiping this for you, Mummy', or 'I like you.' He implies that perhaps Tough has tended to neglect the social or affective aspects of experience because of the predominance of cognitive demands within the school. Wells goes on to remind us of the importance of 'reciprocity' in language development, as adults and children construct a 'shared reality' together. Despite its limitations, Tough's research and the widely used Schools Council materials which have arisen from it, have probably raised the general awareness of a great many teachers on how they might talk with young children with greater purpose and insight.

Frameworks on the functions and uses which have been specifically applied to written language will be dealt with later in this book. In the meantime, it seems reasonable to go along with Smith (1982, p. 15) who suggests that 'Writing can do everything that language in general can do.' Yet it is also worth asking whether writing can fulfil any special functions or at least some functions especially well. Some writers have suggested that the latter is certainly the case. From his studies of the influence of school on cognitive growth Bruner (1972, p. 47) emphasises that 'Writing ... is the training in the use of linguistic contexts that are independent of the immediate referents.' Olson (1977) goes even further. In a densely argued paper, he suggests that written language has a 'bias' towards providing definitions, making assumptions explicit and observing the formal rules of logic. Such a bias has considerable power for building coherent and abstract realities and has formed the basis for the predominant features of Western literate culture and its distinctive modes of thought.

SPOKEN LANGUAGE AND ITS FORMS

Before going on to explore this notion and its implications for teaching writing, it may be helpful to add some details on the nature and development of spoken language, as speech is normally developed well in advance of writing skills and acts as a kind of seed-bed from which writing skills can grow. Initially then, it may be helpful to note some important features of the 'form' of spoken language and its three main 'components', of sounds, words and grammar.

Sounds

The following section deals very briefly with the 'phonological' aspects of pronunciation, the system of sounds in English, rather than the production and transmission of these sounds, which are studied in 'phonetics'. The English language has approximately 40 speech sounds, more specifically called *phonemes*. The phonemes of language are acquired from about the age of nine months (Crystal, 1976, p. 41) as children begin to perceive the differences between sounds and produce them within their normal speech patterns. Evidence suggests that this process of acquisition normally takes until at least the age of seven, with the final consonant phonemes to be acquired being ʃ (as in *sh*ip), tʃ (as in *ch*in), dʒ (as in *j*ump), θ (as in *th*ink) ð (as in *th*em) and ʒ (as in mea*s*ure). (Such phonemic symbols are normally used by linguists in broad transcriptions of speech sounds.) The precise number of phonemes to be acquired will vary between the patterns of pronunciation that we call accents. The accent known as Received Pronunciation (RP), which is generally used, for example, by BBC newsreaders, has 44 phonemes and this is often used as a yardstick in spoken language study and the development of related teaching materials, as is the case with those in the *Breakthrough to Literacy* project (Mackay, 1980). An exaggerated form of this accent also occurs in the speech of members of the royal family and seems to be at least implicitly encouraged at many public schools. Because of its associated status, RP may be felt to be the 'best' or most desirable accent. There is undoubtedly a certain snobbishness about accent differences in Great Britain which has little parallel in many other parts of the world. Nevertheless, from an educational (as opposed to social) point of view, accent differences in themselves are in many ways unimportant. Everyone has an accent of one kind or another, and many accents are regionally based. Accent-based problems in school can occur, of course, when there are major differences in pronunciation between teacher and pupil. These difficulties may crop up in oral reading, when an over-zealous RP-speaking teacher corrects a Lancashire child for pronouncing 'book' as 'buke'. Similarly, a teacher from the north east of England may puzzle Berkshire children by pronouncing 'film' as 'filum'. Providing these differences are approached tolerantly without any exclusive claims to 'correctness', such accent variations in themselves should not be a cause of any significant school-based problems. Whereas RP may be thought of as 'easier to understand' than some regional accents, this is probably because we are more used to hearing it on radio and television, rather than because of any inherent features of RP itself (Trudgill, 1975).

Words

As well as a system of sounds, language comprises a system of meanings (the study of which is called semantics) and in this system vocabulary is widely recognised as playing a central role. There is less agreement among linguists on how other aspects of meaning can be systematically studied within and between sentences and larger language units (Crystal, 1976). There are suggestions that teachers of young children see signs of vocabulary growth as particularly important evidence of language development, especially in written work (DES, 1982a, p. 11). What is perhaps not always appreciated is the systematic nature of this growth. From the early months of children's lives, they are involved in an incremental process of building a store of words, the 'minimum free form units of meaning'. More specifically, minimum units of meaning are known as *morphemes* and the term 'free form' is used to differentiate words from the 'bound form' units of meaning that are represented by morphemes such as the prefix *un-*, the suffix *-ed*, or the plural *-s* which are part of the grammatical development dealt with in the next section. Children often begin by over-extending the application of word labels to the phenomena of the world around them, calling all four-legged creatures 'dog' for instance. More embarrassingly for their parents, they have been known to greet every man with an exclamation of 'da-da!'

From these uncertain beginnings vocabulary development progresses in a variety of ways, with understanding often being in advance of oral use and the latter being in advance of the use of written language, in both children's writing and reading.

The estimation of vocabulary growth in numerical terms is full of difficulties. Estimates of normal vocabulary size in children of particular ages vary enormously, due to the fact that different criteria for 'vocabulary' are used, such as vocabulary items which are spoken, recognised, understood, or defined. Although Dale (1976, p. 192) asserts that 'by his third birthday, the average child has acquired nearly a thousand words', a more illuminating approach to vocabulary growth may be to look at the 'senses' that words can be related to. It is the ability of children to appreciate and put into use appropriate shades of meaning which it is important to try to assess, rather than the totting up of a possibly misleading list of discrete items. It is therefore important to try to identify what these shades of meaning may involve.

One of the central components of vocabulary is the *lexeme*, the idea underlying a set of word forms, such as run, runs, running, ran. Part of the process of vocabulary development is also to distinguish between *homophones*, words which are sounded in the same way but which have different meanings (whether or not they differ in spelling), such as 'hear' and 'here', and *homographs* which are spelled identically but which have different meanings (whether or not they are sounded the same), such as 'spoke' (said) and 'spoke' (of a wheel). These examples are part of the broader field of *homonyms* which, in their absolute form, have identical features of pronunciation, spelling and syntactical equivalence, such as the nouns 'sound' (noise) and 'sound' (an anchorage). Such examples occur widely in English and the Bullock Report (DES, 1975, p. 92) notes how one linguist has suggested that the most common 500 words in the language have between them over 14,000 meanings, thus providing a rich source for exploitation in jokes of all kinds. Experience of such jokes (e.g. Puffin Books, 1978) may be of valuable assistance in what Halliday (1975) has called 'learning how to mean'.

Additional development in vocabulary is concerned with what linguists call *polysemy* and *synonymy*. Polysemy occurs where one word has a range of related meanings as with 'coat' (garment, layer of paint, animal fur, membrane). These senses of the same principal meaning may be varied for figurative effect and can perhaps be a useful indicator of children's linguistic maturity. Synonymy, on the other hand, occurs where words are virtually identical in meaning and therefore easily interchangeable. In a sense, absolute synonyms are likely to cause redundancy, leading to one or more of the alternatives becoming obsolete, and are relatively uncommon. Words which are closely similar, though, are frequently found and may need careful selection within the social context of what is being said or written. Growth in awareness of synonyms is likely to be accompanied by an awareness of antonyms, words which contrast. Gannon and Czerniewska (1980) point out that *antonymy* often has sharper qualities than the rather vague relationships of synonyms. They set out three broad types of antonyms: complementaries, which cannot be scaled (boy – girl, or alive – dead); opposites, which can be scaled (from very rich to very poor); and converse pairs, in which one member of a pair entails the reversal of the other (as in buying and selling).

One final aspect of vocabulary and its development for consideration here is *hyponymy*. This term refers to the relationship of meaning between a superordinate term such as 'bird' and specific terms or hyponyms such as 'sparrow', 'thrush' and 'robin'. The appreciation of such relationships between meanings can form both an important part of a child's growth in understanding the world and a means by which teachers can introduce children to the intricate structure of semantic links which stems from single words.

Grammar

The third principal form of language is grammar, the set of rules which structure the sequences within and between words. Within words, there are morphological rules which govern the possible combinations of morphemes, the minimum units of meaning. As was noted earlier in the chapter, 'free form' morphemes are root words such as *view*. To these, 'bound form' morphemes, which are only 'part words', can be added, such as the prefixes and suffixes in *pre*view, *inter*view, view*er*.

Between words, there are rules of syntax in phrases, clauses, sentences and larger stretches of language. In English, for example, a reporter at a tennis match might say, 'Borg served an ace', whereas in Malagasy a different set of rules govern the positioning of subject, verb and object in a sentence and a reporter would be likely to say, 'Served an ace Borg' (Smith and Wilson, 1979, p. 204). These syntactical rules of a language are learned by listening to and interacting with others. From such early interactions, children construct their own version of the grammatical system of the language, perhaps overgeneralising certain rules on the way ('goed', 'mans', 'badder'). Two distinctive features of this process are that the 'pre-programmed' nature of the human brain may be responsible for some deep-seated grammatical structures being common to all human languages and also for children being able to generate utterances which they have never before encountered (Lyons, 1970, p. 84).

Crystal (1976) suggests that children acquire knowledge of the grammatical system between words through a series of stages:

I   9–18 months, single-element (e.g. dada, gone, more);

II   18 months – 2 years, two-element (e.g. where daddy, gone car, more milk) with a related change in intonation pattern;

III 2–2½ years, three-element sentences (where daddy gone);

IV   2½–3 years, four or more element sentences (Daddy going to work today);

V   3–3½ years, complex sentence structures of more than one clause (e.g. Daddy gone in the car and he taked his coat).

Two other stages follow in which other complexities are developed such as the pronoun system, auxiliary verbs (although understanding the full subtleties of meaning of 'may', 'should' and so on will take several years), a whole range of irregular verbs and nouns, passive forms, sentence connectors (e.g. 'actually', 'however') and so on. This framework is particularly helpful in studying children whose language is unusually slow to develop and it has been extended into a diagnostic framework for studying language disability (Crystal *et al.*, 1976).

In recent years, linguists have come to recognise the importance of inter-personal relationships in fostering language development and the supportive elements of gesture, facial expression and intonation. Differences in intonation, for example, help to add subtleties of meaning to sounds, words and syntax. Consider how the rising or falling 'tunes' convey such subtleties to the phrase 'I see':

(low fall) So it's likely to die? I,see.
(low rise) So you hoped that smoking would help. I,see.
(high fall) So you got there by bus. I'see.
(fall-rise) So you've been talking to that blonde. I'see.

It is also important to recognise differences in dialect which emerge. A dialect is a variation of the same language in a particular region or social group. It includes variation in vocabulary, grammar and, if spoken, accent. The predominant dialect in Great Britain is standard English which is the dialect normally used in published written materials and this can, of course, be spoken in a variety of accents.

Non-standard dialect features are found in the various geographical regions of the country. The standard English form 'I could have smacked her face', for instance, can be heard in Cornish dialect as, 'I could 'ave skat she 'cross the fess.'

Variations from standard English, especially in syntax, have been associated with under-achievement, particularly of children whose families are of West Indian origin and who use forms of non-standard English called Creole. Creole varies from standard English in phonology, vocabulary and grammar – for example, plurals (six boy) and the past tense forms (they go). Such differences have been analysed and discussed by Edwards (1979). Implications for teaching writing will be discussed later, but for the moment it is important to note the warning of the Bullock Report:

> The teacher's ignorance of Creole, and perhaps his traditional attitudes to non-standard forms of English, will tend to make him dismiss Creole features in the West Indian child's speech as incorrect or 'sloppy' English. [In fact, Creole] is recognised by linguists as being a well developed language, with a sound system, grammar and vocabulary of its own and capable – like other forms of English – of being used expressively and richly (DES, 1975, p. 287).

FROM TALKING TO WRITING

From the previous sections, it can be seen that children normally bring a very wide-ranging linguistic competence and repertoire to school, on which the development of writing can be based, and which has been summarised by Roger Brown (1968, p. v) in an almost celebratory way.

Most children, by the time they are ready to begin school, know the full contents of an introductory book in transformational grammar. One such text is a bit more than 400 pages long and it covers declaratives and interrogatives, affirmatives and negatives, actives and passives, simple sentences, conjoined sentences and some kinds of embedded sentences. The preschool child knows all this.

Brown goes on to acknowledge that this knowledge is not explicit and that children are not able to 'formulate' their grammatical knowledge or do it justice in acts of communication.

Nevertheless, Brown's words are borne out by the findings of a ten-year study of the language development of 120 Bristol children undertaken by Gordon Wells.

The most impressive finding from the research is the amount that all children have learned about communicating through language by the time they go to school. Almost every child has mastered the basic meanings and grammar of the language of his community and is using language for a variety of purposes in his interaction with the people in his immediate surroundings (Wells, 1981a).

Despite such a rich language competence, however, children will often have some difficulty in adjusting to the language demands of the school in the production of written language. To try to understand the nature of these difficulties, it is important to examine the nature of the process of writing in itself. A useful way of beginning such an examination is to summarise the main differences between reading and writing.

THE DIFFERENCES BETWEEN READING AND WRITING

These differences are related to each other in complex ways but point towards some of the difficulties which children may experience in becoming 'writers'. There are the more obvious differences: that writing is made of marks on paper, not sounds in the air; writing follows certain directional conventions left to right down the page and uses punctuation of various sorts which have little comparability with pauses in speech. There are also differences which have more profound implications for children learning to write: the written symbols which represent words have to be made up by the relatively slow procedure of putting together the forty-three shapes of the upper and lower-case alphabet; these words will have to be arranged in formally constructed sentences with appropriate spacing and neither of these features have direct equivalents in speech. Moreover, the writer does not normally have the 'respondent' that the speaker will face and who provides the cues, facial expression, and interruption which indicates whether the spoken message is being understood.

As Thornton (1980, p. 11) reminds us,

The writer . . . faces a piece of paper that will be read in another place at some future time. A speaker can alter, cancel, start again. A writer can do this at the drafting stage, but at some point he must let go of his writing, and, once he has, he can do nothing to alter what he has written. It stands, or falls, by itself. It is not, like spontaneous speech, inextricably bound to the context in which it occurs.

THE PROCESS OF WRITING: COMPOSING, TRANSCRIBING, REVIEWING

The process of channelling spoken language competence into the production of writing can be seen as being made up of three basic components: 'composing', 'transcribing' and 'reviewing'. Put even more simply they represent pre-writing, writing and rewriting. The following section deals with each of these three and then considers some of their interrelationships. To add a practical but underused source, I have referred to the words of well known writers on their perceptions of the writing process and the cycle of decisions on 'what to write', 'how to write it' and 'how to improve what has been written'. They can be represented diagrammatically as follows:

Composing

In this chapter, each of these components will be dealt with separately, although the complex nature of their interrelationships needs to be continually borne in mind. Of the three, transcription has generally received more attention in educational studies and in teaching, even though it can be said that composing plays the fundamental role in written language production. In fact, the relationship between composing and transcribing is often complex (Flower and Hayes, 1980), but because of its relative neglect it may be worth examining the nature of composing in the writing process in particular detail here. In a book which deals with research on composing, Cooper and Odell (1978, p. xi) point out, 'what we have needed for decades . . . is a period of vigorous research on written discourse and the composing process.' Later in their book, they go on to review some of the problems of gaining knowledge of the composing process, including the inaccessibility of the 'data': 'even highly competent professional writers have difficulty articulating the basis on which they make decisions about what they say and how they say it' (Odell *et al.*, 1978, p. 6). Perhaps the relative influences of different factors which influence composing can only be judged properly by directly intervening in the writing process as it is going on, rather than asking people 'what they did' after they have finished writing.

It is this approach which has been largely adopted by Bereiter and his colleagues in a series of original studies at the Ontario Institute for Studies in Education. In a recent paper which draws together the findings of a number of research studies, Bereiter and Scardamalia (1982) confirm that learning to write involves several major psychological adjustments: from oral to graphic expression; from face to face communication to communication with a remote audience; and from the use of a language production system dependent on inputs from a 'conversational partner' to the development of a system capable of functioning autonomously.

In concentrating upon the third of these adjustments they argue that it is not enough to know what needs to be learned but that it is necessary to probe beneath this knowledge to examine the difficulties that are encountered in learning it. The experiments of Bereiter and Scardamalia have particularly focused on 'procedural facilitation' – ways in which children can be helped in the development of this autonomous language system. As yet the published research findings have not dealt with attempts to increase the all-round performance of children's writing. Instead, the work has concentrated on which mental operations appear to be most susceptible to facilitative intervention by sympathetic adults. These are dealt with in chapter 9.

Bereiter and Scardamalia suggest that for the purposes of analysis the composing process can be broken down into a number of discrete cognitive tasks: searching the mind for suitable content and continually relating the constituent parts of the written text to the projected whole.

Finding content for writing rather than the language to express it seems to be a problem both for children and adults alike (Bereiter and Scardamalia, 1982; Elbow, 1973; Odell et al., 1978). The search for content can be seen as consisting of two parts: generating one's knowledge about a particular topic and then selecting from this available content in order to meet the demands of a particular writing task. The store of information within the brain on which a writer can draw is made up of an accumulation of meanings constructed from experience. There is a great deal of evidence that this information is stored systematically in the long-term memory (Lindsay and Norman, 1972). It is common for many people to 'forget what they know' and then have the recall of a whole network of memories triggered off by a single incident, experience or activity.

One central task for the writer, then, is to consider what seems to be the best technique for setting off these recall and selection procedures. Reports of adult writers suggest that such 'techniques' may include a whole range of idiosyncracies from going for walks to sniffing rotten apples (Burgess et al., 1973, p. 10). From these beginnings, a plan may well evolve which perhaps 'models' the intended written structure (as in an outline), abstracts its main features (like listing the main points) or merely involves scribbling down 'bunches of ideas' (Flower and Hayes, 1980). Notice the kinds of recall and planning techniques used by Laurie Lee in beginning work on Cider with Rosie, the story of his early life in a Cotswold village.

Notice, too, the image that he selects to convey this process: designing and furnishing a house.

> . . . If a book is to stand, one must first choose its shape – the house that the tale will inhabit. One lays out the rooms for the necessary chapters, then starts wondering about the furniture. The moment before writing is perhaps the most harrowing of all, pacing the empty rooms, knowing that what goes in there can belong nowhere else, yet not at all sure where to find it. There are roofless books in all of us, books without walls and books full of lumber. I realized quite soon, when writing my own, that I had enough furniture to fill a town (Lee, 1977, pp. 50–1).

An additional problem in composing is the continual need to relate selected content to the overall whole, what Bereiter and Scardamalia (1982) call 'shifting from local to whole-text planning'. Again the difficulties in this aspect of writing emanate partly from its fundamental difference from speech which progresses in a series of short 'exchanges', which normally lack the predictable 'whole' on which any kind of master-plan could be based.

A major resource for whole-text planning will be the writer's knowledge of the established patterns of various written 'discourse structures' such as stories, scientific reports, instructions or arguments. The term 'schema' is increasingly being used to apply to this kind of knowledge which provides a tacit framework for interpreting new experience (Anderson, 1977). It has been suggested that a schema, such as a 'story grammar', can provide considerable aid to the comprehension of stories. As Pearson and Johnson (1978, p. 17) put it, '. . . there is something very predictable about the structure of events in a fairy tale, folktale, or fable, even when we have not heard or read the particular story in question'. It seems very likely that this kind of tacit resource can be very helpful in the writing of such stories, too. Applebee (1978) points out that children build upon their pre-sleep 'monologues' at two-and-a-half and by five or six are frequently incorporating features of a 'conventional, culturally provided frame of the story mode' such as formal opening and closing phrases, the use of the past tense and the acceptance of make-believe characters in their stories.

However, the growth of awareness of other discourse 'grammars' such as those related to persuasion or argument seems to develop considerably later and may not be particularly mature even in higher education students (Beard, 1978), despite their exposure to various models in their previous studies.

Transcribing

The process of converting the results of composition into coherent marks on the page is variously called transcribing, translating or articulating (Frederiksen and Dominic, 1981, p. 4). Here the first term is used, as it seems to best convey the use of the network of skills which Smith (1982) likens to a 'tapestry'. This network is made up of the skills of handwriting, spelling, selection and use of vocabulary, punctuation, constructing appropriate sentence structures, linking them with each other and arranging them in appropriate patterns of discourse. To pay attention to all these skills within the same activity is obviously very challenging for children and Scardamalia (1981) suggests that the process of planning and reviewing may be relatively late to develop in young children because they already have so much to which to give attention in a writing task.

In transcription, too, the writing task involves a number of activities which can be separated into discrete areas for analysis and study. These include physical co-ordination and directionality (left to right movements, top to bottom down the page) as well as the various skills listed above.

All these stem from the particular nature of the creativity of written language – the act of representing language in a permanent form. A recognition of the psychological significance of this is found in a thorough analysis of the physiological influences on the learning of writing by Ajuriaguerra and Auzias (1975, p. 312):

> It is speech and motion . . . It is . . . mastery of a tool and a new method of handling language . . . Of all manual skills, writing allows the child least liberty, while affording him the greatest satisfaction, because it can provide an indelible trace of what language can express.

See how this deep-seated awareness of the construction of a permanent form of language lies at the heart of the work of the celebrated poet Philip Larkin:

> I write poems to preserve things I have seen/thought/felt (if I may so indicate a composite and complex experience) both for myself and for others, though I feel that my prime responsibility is to the experience itself, which I am trying to keep from oblivion for its own sake. Why I should do this I have no idea but I think the impulse to preserve lies at the bottom of all art (in King, 1979, p. 2).

In some ways it might be felt that the transcribing part of writing involves a direct application of the knowledge and skills of language, its sounds, words and grammar. This would be an over-simplified view of writing, however. As will be shown later, there are important cognitive adjustments to be made in the perceptions of language when these spoken utterances are transcribed into written forms. Spelling involves far more than merely representing phonemes by their equivalent letters; words have to be precisely selected from the appropriate semantic field; the grammar of writing is typically far more 'formal' than the loosely-chained structures of speech.

Reviewing

The reviewing process is perhaps the most neglected aspect in the teaching of writing. Conducting any kind of review must assume that the writing so far completed can be altered, either by minor editing or major redrafting. There are indications that the role and importance of such reappraisals are not widely appreciated.

After working with a large number of college-age 'Basic Writing' students, Shaughnessy (1977, p. 79) reports that those who are not aware of the role and importance of reviewing in writing

> tend to think that the point in writing is to get everything right the first time and that the need to change things is the mark of the amateur. (Thus a student who saw a manuscript page of Richard Wright's *Native Son*, with all its original deletions and substitutions, concluded that Wright couldn't have been much of a writer if he made all those 'mistakes'.)

There are good reasons for suspecting that over-conscientious teachers may be responsible for this state of affairs, for at least two main reasons. One is a failure to allow for appropriate drafting procedures to take place in school and to insist on 'fair copies' from the start. Children who regularly cross things out or use a rubber may be seen as showing signs of irritating weakness. Such an over-zealous approach may result in an omnipresent psychological constraint:

> Sitting on the shoulder of many writers is the wraith of a school teacher, waiting to jump on every fault of punctuation or spelling, on every infelicity of expression (Smith, 1982, p. 132).

Teachers may be responsible for not encouraging the reviewing of writing for a second reason, that they themselves have not appreciated its role in writing. This appreciation may only come from a critical self-examination of their own approaches to writing tasks which have some degree of challenge or uncertainty. This possibility is offered by Emig (1971) who concludes that, unless this is undertaken, teachers are in danger of under-conceptualising and over-simplifying the nature of the writing process.

Reviewing and redrafting are certainly at the centre of Penelope Lively's work, an author who not only has won a Carnegie Medal for her children's novel *The Ghost of Thomas Kempe* but also has written successful adult novels, including *The Road to Lichfield* which was short-listed for the Booker Prize in 1977. When visiting the class of primary school children I was teaching a few years ago, she described the writing of a novel like this:

> I write it once and then I put it away and then I write it again . . . because you don't write a book just straight off like that, you know. It's a piece of work that's got to be absolutely right, as right as you can get it. So when you've written it, it's not finished. Then you write it all over again. And then you write it again. And then you go back and write the most important bits again. It's like that, you see.

When 'reviewing activities' of this kind are considered in detail, it becomes clear that there are no clear divisions between composing, transcribing and reviewing. Each may inform the others in ways so complex that Hayes and Flower (1980, p. 33) feel that from their research a writer resembles 'a very busy switchboard operator trying to juggle a number of demands on her attention and constraints on what she can do'.

The suggestion that there is a complex evolving interaction between what is written and the writing of it, is supported by a range of quotations from professional writers brought together by Murray (1978) and which include the following:

'How do I know what I think until I see what I say?' (E. M. Forster)

'As you continue writing and rewriting, you begin to see possibilities you hadn't seen before. Writing a poem is always a process of discovery.' (Robert Hayden)

'Writing and rewriting are a constant search for what one is saying.' (John Updike)

THE WRITING CONTEXT

Although it is clearly very important to explore some of the dynamics of the central components of the writing process, it is also important to acknowledge the influence of certain factors in the immediate context, such as aim, audience, content and mode (which were introduced in the first chapter). Several of the more significant of these factors are set out below in an expanded version of the earlier diagram (page 28).

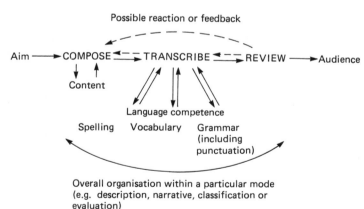

Such a diagram is still inevitably simplified and a number of other important factors are still not properly dealt with in it. The writer's values, motivation, self-concept as a writer and store of world knowledge can be very influential in the writing process. Furthermore, the diagram does not deal effectively with the 'register' of language use – that is, the style of language appropriate for a particular set of circumstances. A register is influenced by such features as the choice of subject matter, the purpose and nature of language used and the kind of social relationship between language producer and audience (Gregory and Carroll, 1978). Together they will be manifested in a range of subtle choices in vocabulary and grammar and contribute to a general 'air' of relative formality or informality.

Nevertheless, the above diagram does locate some of the principal aspects of the writing process and therefore can be used as a basis for considering the available theoretical frameworks on the general development of children's writing. This is what is attempted in the next chapter.

4 Dimensions of writing development

Having discussed the process and the components of writing, we now need to consider how writing develops in the primary and middle school years. From the discussion in the last chapter, it will be clear that an assessment of the development of a child's writing can be approached along a number of different dimensions. In a recent paper, Shuy (1981) has identified five 'language systems' involved in writing: spelling and punctuation; morphology; vocabulary; syntax; and written discourse. He suggests that, in learning to write, syntactical development occurs later than the other systems. Shuy argues that the most important development in the ability to write effectively for a variety of circumstances will occur at the level of discourse, involving the organisation of writing, the cohesion between its parts, and the variation of written language in dialects, registers and genres.

There are several other ways in which the development of writing in children can be studied. Some of the main dimensions are indicated in four important publications: Harpin's (1976) research into basic linguistic features, Moffett's (1968) model of levels of abstraction, the research of Wilkinson *et al.* (1980) into a number of features of 'personal' development in writing, and Bereiter's (1980) model of cognitive stages in writing development evolved from his continuing research.

LINGUISTIC DEVELOPMENT

Harpin (1976) tells us about evidence on the development of several linguistic features from the writing of a sample of junior school children who completed both 'creative' and 'factual' writing tasks. The research concentrated on word counts, vocabulary and syntactical structures (sentence length, clause length, type and number of subordinate units). As Harpin acknowledges, the design and administration of such measures is beset with difficulties ('St Francis got back and he had some followers as well' – one sentence or two?). Yet despite such uncertainties some interesting possibilities emerged from the research. In a series of word counts from the writing of nearly 300 children, the results suggested that by the fourth year of the junior school children were beginning to reduce the general rate of advance in writing output. Together with other evidence, this suggested a stage of consolidation in which there was perhaps greater economy and more deliberate shaping of their writing.

Harpin's research did not deal directly with vocabulary because of the kinds of difficulty in assessing vocabulary growth which were dealt with in the last chapter. But he does put forward a possible way of gaining some indications of range and flexibility of vocabulary. The number of different words ('types') in a piece of writing can be expressed as a proportion of the total number of words ('tokens'), to give a 'type-token ratio' (TTR). Comparisons can be made between succeeding segments of 50 or 100 words from a piece of writing. Harpin's review of available evidence suggests that 'for children aged seven to 11, ratios for the first 100 words tend to range in value from 0.45–0.70 . . . The sharper the drop in TTR after the first 100 words, the less diverse a child's vocabulary resources are likely to be' (Harpin, 1976, p. 56). Therefore a low TTR will suggest that children are tending to use the same words over and over again.

In examining the development of syntactical structures, Harpin presents the greatest number of findings and anyone interested in this area would find it valuable to consult both the detail of the results and Harpin's cautious commentary. Although it was not a central focus in the research, Harpin does outline some possible features of the growth in children's use of conjunctions. Part of the growing maturity of writing is to accommodate not only alternatives to 'and', but also to express the subtleties of meaning which other 'near equivalents' can allow.

The wind blew and the snowflakes fell → As the wind blew, the snowflakes fell. (additional, simultaneous detail)

The autumn came and the leaves fell → Because the autumn came, the leaves fell. (cause–effect relationship)

He finished work and went to bed → After he finished work he went to bed. (time sequence)

(adapted from Harpin, 1976, p. 68)

Harpin provides some interesting details on developments in the use of clauses, units of language which contain a finite verb or verb phrase. Although a variety of new approaches to grammatical analysis have developed in recent years, the adoption of some traditional terms may help clarify a summary of Harpin's evidence. Clauses can be 'independent' and act as 'simple' sentences on their own ('The band began to play' or 'Everyone enjoyed the music'), or can be 'dependent' or subordinate ('When the audience had arrived' . . .). Compound sentences are made up of two independent clauses ('The band began to play and everyone enjoyed the music'). Complex sentences consist of an independent clause and at least one subordinate clause ('When the audience had arrived, the band began to play').

Subordinate clauses can be broadly classified according to their function, as with noun clauses, adverbial clauses, or adjectival clauses, and these classifications are used in Harpin's results.

The results from the study of nearly 7,000 samples of writing collected over six terms from the 290 children showed that nearly all the children used some subordinate clauses, although in a few cases they were used very infrequently. An analysis of the clauses showed a preponderance of the use of adverbial and noun clauses over adjectival ones.

There was no sign of any particular kinds of development in the use of adverbial clauses, in which clauses of time predominated throughout the junior age range. This predominance seems to be a reflection of the preference for the narrative mode in children's writing (After/While/When/he went for a walk . . .). Other kinds of adverbial clause made up only 11 per cent of the total number of subordinate clauses, the most frequently used being clauses of cause, condition, place and result.

In the analysis of the use of noun and adjectival clauses, there were signs of developmental trends. Noun clauses decreased as a percentage of all subordination between Year 1 (46 per cent) and Year 4 (34 per cent). Within this range there was a definite shift from direct to indirect speech, although generally noun clauses were predominantly used as the objects of sentences (e.g. 'She said that she was going to the dance'), and very rarely in others ways, such as subject (e.g. 'What he wants is help').

The decline in the use of noun clauses was accompanied by a greater use of adjectival clauses ('The lady who was sitting in the bus' . . .), the latter making up 11 per cent of the total number of subordinate clauses in Year 1 and 22 per cent in Year 4. Harpin suggests that this relative increase might be a reflection of children's increasing mastery of the use of potentially confusing relative pronouns (who, whom, which, that), and a growing interest in the possibilities of additional 'decorative' structures, especially in descriptions.

DEVELOPMENT IN LEVELS OF ABSTRACTION

The developmental model of Moffett (1968) contrasts with Harpin's framework, in that it does not deal with linguistic aspects of writing but with the 'levels of abstraction' which writing reveals. In short, these levels are:
    recording;
    reporting;
    generalising;
    theorising.
The concept of abstraction is useful to Moffett because he can apply it equally well to mental development and to the structure of discourse (Moffett, 1968, p. 18). An important part of abstracting is 'decentering':

> Differentiating among modes of discourse, registers of speech, kinds of audiences is essentially a matter of decentering, of seeing alternatives, of standing in others' shoes, of knowing that one has a private or local point of view and knowledge structure (Moffett, 1968, p. 57).

Moffett does not include any original research evidence or examples of children's writing in his book, but his suggested levels of abstraction have recently been adopted in an LEA booklet of suggestions for a policy for writing development from eight to 13 by Harris and Kay (1981). They argue that Moffett's 'generalising' and 'theorising' levels are difficult for children to deal with in writing because these levels lack the time-related organisation which is so helpful in the recording and reporting of, for example, stories, autobiographical writing and reports of visits or experiments.

PERSONAL DEVELOPMENT

Wilkinson *et al.* (1980) also partially adopted Moffett's model in their research on developmental features in a sample of seven- to 13-year-old children in Crediton, Devon, although their research framework is different from that of Harpin reviewed above, examining not only 'style' but also cognitive (incorporating Moffett's levels), affective and moral development. Wilkinson *et al.* argue that examining writing development by counting words, sentence length or clause type neglects personal development and the construction of meaning. At the centre of this research is the recognition of the child as the communicating being. Consequently the research in the 'Crediton Project' established and applied models in additional areas. The principal features of the models are as follows:

cognitive	*affective*	*moral*	*stylistic*
description	awareness of self	anomy	simple literal affirmative sentence,
interpretation	awareness of others	heteronomy	growth in syntax, verbal competence,
generalisation	empathy with reader	socionomy	organisation, cohesion,
speculation	sense of environment awareness of reality	autonomy	reader awareness, appropriateness, effectiveness

These models were then selectively used in a study of the writing of about 150 children aged seven, ten and 13 on four written tasks: an autobiographical narrative, an explanation, a fictional story and a persuasive argument.

Comments on the detailed findings have to be very selective so perhaps it is best to note what the research sample indicated about achievements at 13+, to give a perspective on what middle school children are capable of.

In cognitive development, 13-year-olds were showing that they could abstract, summarise, evaluate and generalise, supporting generalisations with concrete evidence. Some were beginning to project hypotheses, something which none of the ten-year-old children were apparently doing in their writing.

The study of children's affective development in writing suggested a movement from literal statements with no affective elements at seven through to greater psychological authenticity at 13, where more realistic themes are used together with the use of introspection which was not found in ten-year-olds' writing. Even here, though, emotion is not always brought into writing in explicit ways but obliquely through characters' behaviour. At ten there is greater explicitness of emotion to deepen the theme and in the use of environmental details to intensify moods or attitudes, often through fantasy narratives with mass media-based themes.

The findings on moral development needed to be very cautious because they were based on inferences from verbal judgements and not from observed behaviour. With this reservation in mind, Wilkinson *et al.* report that no evidence was found of judgement in terms of abstract universal principles, although this was to be expected, given the age-range studied. Generally the findings of earlier research by Kohlberg was confirmed, that between seven and 13 children shift from a tendency to make judgements in terms of punishments or rewards (*heteronomy*), to a tendency to judge in terms of the maintenance of good relationships (*socionomy*), to a stage where principles of fairness and intention were drawn upon (*autonomy*).

The findings on style confirmed the anticipated move from partial to complete organisation in terms of syntax and verbal competence; organisation and cohesion; reader awareness and appropriateness; and overall effectiveness. Although much of this is to be expected, it is nevertheless an unusually wide-ranging investigation, going far beyond the more traditional focus of attention on vocabulary, spelling, or punctuation. There is also a thoughtful caveat on possible responses to 'stock expressions' and 'over-writing'.

Often the writers' very eagerness to write well can produce an impression of 'insincerity' where the language seems second-hand and the emotions expressed exaggerated. Sometimes the reaching out for metaphorical language, even the 'objective correlative' of the story, seems to result in exaggerated or melodramatic emotion. Where there is a specific literary model this feeling of overwriting, and of second-hand emotion may be particularly strong. It behoves us to be careful however . . . . The writer works through the stock language and stereotype perceptions associated with it to an individual perception expressed in individual terms. This is a hard won end – we can scarcely expect children to have gone through the process by the age of thirteen (Wilkinson *et al.*, 1980, p. 221).

In general, then, there was a good deal of evidence to support the four models although Wilkinson *et al.* warn of their provisional nature, particularly those concerned with affect and style, as there was very little previous research work to draw upon. Finally, there are two general findings to note which are especially significant for the purposes of the present discussion.

One is that, from the evidence, Wilkinson and his colleagues felt that the overall performance in the 'discursive' tasks, the persuasive argument and the explanation, was weaker than that in the personal writing of the autobiography and the story. Many children used a narrative mode for the latter two, but also tried to adopt it inappropriately for the argument and explanation. There seemed to be a general lack of awareness on how to construct appropriate writing for these purposes, perhaps because of their unfamiliarity with models for these kinds of writing, although the difficulty of the task itself should not be underestimated.

The second is that various syntactical items which had not appeared in Harpin's (1976) samples were consistently found in the Crediton results, such as clauses of condition, modal verbs (for example, could, may), and expressions of tentativeness. Wilkinson feels that such differences are due to the nature of the writing tasks required of the children: Wilkinson's tasks required persuasive argument; Harpin's did not. This raises the crucial issue of the influence of the context of writing, which, together with the evidence on discursive writing, will be returned to in chapters 7 and 8.

COGNITIVE STAGES IN WRITING DEVELOPMENT

The final longitudinal framework to be examined here is that of Bereiter (1980). Bereiter sets out five basic stages of writing, within an 'applied cognitive–developmental framework'. The term 'stage' is used in a more limited sense than the way Piaget uses it, but helps emphasise that writing

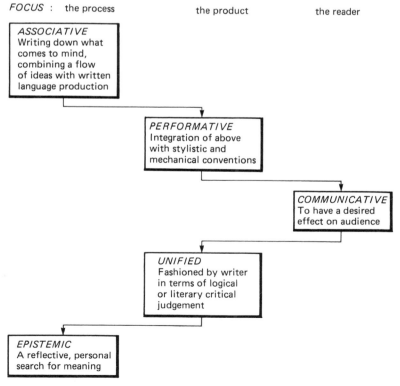

FOCUS : the process   the product   the reader

ASSOCIATIVE
Writing down what comes to mind, combining a flow of ideas with written language production

PERFORMATIVE
Integration of above with stylistic and mechanical conventions

COMMUNICATIVE
To have a desired effect on audience

UNIFIED
Fashioned by writer in terms of logical or literary critical judgement

EPISTEMIC
A reflective, personal search for meaning

(after Bereiter, 1980, p. 84)

development may involve successively discrete forms of cognitive organisation. Each stage will require some readjustment of the process used, rather than the mere addition of new skills to it.

Bereiter warns that the stages which he has identified from a series of research studies may not be universal or have a necessary order, but he feels that they have a seemingly 'natural' order to them, in that making one stage automatic greatly facilitates progress to the next stage.

One particularly interesting feature of the model is that it allows for differing emphases of conscious 'focus'. Associative and epistemic writing are focused on the 'process' of writing, performative and unified on the product and communicative on the reader. Bereiter suggests that traditional teaching methods based on exercises and teacher correction are devoted to moving students from associative to performative writing. Such a narrow focus neglects a number of valuable possibilities:

> . . . Attaining a degree of mastery over stylistic conventions leads in turn to the discovery that writing can be used to affect the reader – that it can direct, inform, amuse, move emotionally and so on. Thence emerges the communicative stage. Once students start writing for readers, it becomes a natural next step for them to start reading their own writing, which sets in motion the writing–reading feedback loop on which the stage of unified writing depends. Once this feedback loop is functioning well, it will be natural to discover that it leads not only to improved writing but also to improved understanding – that the loop constitutes a kind of dialogue with oneself. Thus may emerge the final, epistemic stage of writing development (Bereiter, 1980, p. 89).

Taken together, the studies of Harpin, Moffett, Wilkinson *et al.* and Bereiter highlight several complementary points. One is that, judging from Harpin's research in particular, there do seem to be predictable patterns of linguistic development in children's writing. How far the rate of development can be increased by sensitive teacher intervention has yet to be properly researched. Certainly any research of this kind would also need to make due allowance for the development of the person engaged in the writing tasks.

This introduces a second point. Wilkinson's work helps to counteract the tendency of specialised linguistic research to neglect the personal construction of meaning and the associated affective and moral growth within the person. (Not that Harpin's work was necessarily guilty of such neglect.) Wilkinson's research design was very ambitious and laid great store by the validity of the inferences made by the research team. Future work of this kind would probably benefit from an increase in the data collected on the children themselves, including interviews with them, following the lead of Southgate *et al.* (1981) in their research into children's views on reading. In general, though, the contribution of Wilkinson's research is an important humanistic one.

Although Moffett's work has been incorporated into Wilkinson's model, his focus on 'decentering' also can be linked with Bereiter's framework, which seems to assume greater realisation by the writer of alternative conventions, arguments and forms. Together, these reports and arguments provide some kind of general picture of young writers increasing their linguistic resources and their abilities to decentre, with this process being accompanied by some features of emotional and moral growth.

Yet the picture is far from complete. The growth patterns of several of the aspects identified by Shuy (1981) and listed earlier in this chapter remain under-researched, especially in respect of the general organisation of the writing, within different registers and modes. Much has still to be done to delineate an overall pattern of growth of writing skills, and its relationship to curriculum provision. The brief comparison of the findings of Harpin and Wilkinson suggests that this relationship is very worthy of further exploration.

Finally, Bereiter's work underlines the importance of aims in writing. His framework carries with it an increasing differentiation of aims which may be adopted to transcend or bypass some stages in his model. He cites the work of Kohl (1967) as indication of children who are not proficient at either 'performative' or 'communicative' writing being able to undertake 'unified' writing, which is aesthetically satisfying. Similarly the ideas of Elbow (1973) can be used to show how 'epistemic' writing may be a helpful goal for people 'hung up' on 'performative' writing. The intention which one brings to the task helps carry one through the difficulties encountered in it. The next chapter takes up the central role of aims, but first examines the different frameworks of writing 'types' within which books on children's writing have been written in the last forty years or so.

5   Different types of writing

As pointed out at the end of chapter 2, there is a wide range of verbal labels used to describe different types of writing. These labels are often used without a full definition of their precise meaning or the relationships between them. This chapter examines the various frameworks of labels which are commonly used and establishes one reasonably coherent and comprehensive framework on which much of the rest of this book is based.

Books for teachers on children's writing tend to use simple frameworks of writing types rather than tracing features of 'longitudinal' development such as those discussed in the last chapter. Let us begin by looking at some of these frameworks before going on to consider those used in definitive research projects or discourse studies.

The classification of writing types can be related to any of the four parameters set out in chapters 1 and 3: aim, audience, content, or mode. As Harpin (1976, p. 39) points out, other classifications might be also based on writer–audience relationships such as the intimate-casual-consultative-formal-frozen styles suggested by Joos (1962), or simply by graphical 'form', for instance prose/poetry or essay/composition. This chapter will show that where publications on children's writing have used explicit classifications they have tended to be based on mode or form, often neglecting the aims of writing tasks.

The books discussed here have all been written for primary school teachers in the four decades since the second world war. For a survey extending back to the earlier part of the twentieth century and beyond, a useful source is Harpin (1976). Some details of the structure and content of each book have been given to help show what kinds of classroom practices might stem from them. Although a number of these books are now out of print, they can still be found on the bookshelves of school staffrooms as well as in colleges and universities concerned with primary education, and the following commentary might help draw attention to the particular features of each which might be adopted for future curriculum planning.

Cutforth's (1954) *English in the Primary School* was particularly concerned to encourage teachers to allow children to base their writing on real experience, especially local studies. This former member of HM Inspectorate argues against the use of exercise books (although acknowledging the value of rough note-books and their use as 'mental workshops'). Instead, he recommends that teachers and children should make their own books in which children can set down clearly and simply pieces of information that they have found out by themselves and from which poetry writing can emerge. Cutforth also points out the effectiveness of a 'newsroom' approach in the classroom, where 'newspapers', correspondence on visits, talks, quizzes and arguments are the mainstream activities. This approach relates writing closely to the oral foundations which Cutforth sees as so important in harnessing the possibilities of English as part of the whole of education, rather than as a separate subject.

Gagg's (1955) *Teaching Written English* shares many of Cutforth's priorities although its style is more idiosyncratic. Gagg begins by saying that traditionally the 'second R' has been misguidedly taught, 'means' (punctuation, spelling, grammar, neatness) being taught without due recognition of 'aims', that is the purpose, interest and content of writing. Gagg's book outlines a range of practical ideas in which the aims can be properly incorporated. From a brief description of the stages by which writing is first taught, the book deals with a variety of writing types, such as displays, books, letters, stories, study writing, newspapers and magazines, plays and poems. The notion of 'study writing' is an interesting one, for it represents a concern for the individual use of textbooks in 'study topics' which at that time was probably not as widespread as it has become since.

Both these books are notable for the lack of any mention of providing children with direct 'stimuli' for writing and there is little sign of these being mentioned in books for teachers before Pym's (1956) *Free Writing*. Beginning as a means of giving confidence to Postgraduate Certificate in Education (PGCE) students at Bristol University for the writing of course-work essays, it was adapted for 11 + papers and was later taken up in a series of experiments in Wiltshire schools. Pym's account of the work identifies the essential features: many students were 'stimulated' by various starting points, often in the form of a sense-experience, to write fluently. The consequent feeling of 'liberation' enlivened their essay work because 'it seemed that the "essay" regarded as a school exercise, practised to pass an examination and operated almost as an external mechanism, was connected with what someone else wanted and not with what they themselves had to say' (Pym, 1956, p. 11). In some ways the label 'free' writing is a misnomer because the approach was 'chiefly concerned with writing from a starting point, not with a free choice of subject' (ibid., p. 122). In various ways, it was to dominate the teacher publications of the 'sixties. Before then, though, a book which took a similar but distinctly separate line was published, Hourd and Cooper's (1959) *Coming into Their Own*.

This book describes and analyses the poetry written by ten-year-old children who were regularly read nursery rhymes and poems from a wide range of sources by their headmistress, Gertrude Cooper, and then given the opportunity to write their own in home-made and decorated books. The main commentary on the children's work is provided by Marjorie Hourd who examines what the poems suggest about children's ideas on the outer world, the supernatural, death and destruction, good and bad and other psychological themes. She goes on to discuss issues such as children's handling of the verse form, plagiarism, rewriting and what children's poetry can suggest about children's personal development. The book as a whole has unusual psychological and literary depth for its time, although in the following ten years not as many writers built upon it as might have been expected. While later books share Hourd and Cooper's concern for releasing children's potential for writing in imaginative and poetic ways, they use the more direct 'starting point' approaches of Pym rather than Cooper and Hourd's perspective. The latter was more concerned with the creation of a 'literary environment', within which children were encouraged to experiment in verse forms with whatever subject matter they felt their writing drawn towards.

'Starting points' were very much part of Margaret Langdon's (1961) work with older elementary school children on 'intensive writing'. In a book called *Let the Children Write*, she describes how she encouraged 12- and 13-year-olds to concentrate on what Wordsworth called 'emotion recollected in tranquility'. The 'intensive writing' approach was to encourage the children 'to recollect an emotional experience and express it briefly, simply and with honesty' (Langdon, 1961, p. 7). Inspired by the 'modern verse' of Dylan Thomas, D. H. Lawrence and T. S. Eliot, Langdon initially asked children to write about an imaginary spider on the classroom wall. She guided them, line by line, to write about their initial reaction, the spider's body, to use three adjectives to describe its legs, the web and so on. In subsequent sessions she asked the children to write about 'being alone in a room during a storm' and 'fear', and went on to using such starting points as the direct experience of walking across the school field on a spring day and also using Lawrence's poem 'Snake' for stimulating writing on any creature of the children's choice.

An article on the children's writing on these and other topics was later published in an educational paper and brought letters from all over the country and from different parts of the world. There were clearly many teachers ready to try this new teacher-directed stimulus approach to enliven children's writing and encourage them to link emotion with the form of the words on the page.

Within this tradition, three years later another book for teachers was published, Alec Clegg's (1964) *The Excitement of Writing*. This book is essentially an anthology of children's writing from the West Riding of Yorkshire with a commentary by the teachers involved and Clegg, then Chief Education Officer. Clegg distinguishes between writing which is 'recording' and writing which is 'personal', and argues against books of English exercises which he sees as being 'harmful'. The book is largely devoted to personal writing, which includes poetry, expressive prose, writing about personal experiences, impressions or imaginings (Clegg, 1964, p. 5). The precise contexts of the writing obviously varied from teacher to teacher, but generally there is an emphasis on writing from experience, both that provided by the teacher in planning the curriculum and also the experience of life outside school, including the unprepossessing environment of pit-heads and back-to-back housing. In their commentaries, some teachers were becoming aware that the teaching of writing deserved attention to aims and readership, but most seem to be preoccupied by the possibilities of language form. Only a few of the teachers use the words 'creative writing' although it is this phrase, rather than 'personal', that Denys Thompson uses in his foreword to the book, from which, he suggests, it emerges that

> 'creative' writing in schools is neither a luxury allowed by indulgent teachers, nor a form of psychotherapy, but a mode of expression that children practise readily, deriving confidence and fluency from it, and stocking up for their 'recording' work when it is called for in history, science and so on (in Clegg, 1964, p. viii).

Within three years a spate of books for teachers had appeared, in which the emphasis was predominantly on 'creative' writing. One book of this time which did not follow this trend was Joan Dean's (1968) *Reading, Writing and Talking*. This book makes the distinction between 'factual' writing (seen in its extreme in the report of a scientific experiment) and 'personal' writing (taken to its extreme in poetry). Perhaps the best known of the 'creative writing' books is Barry Maybury's (1967) *Creative Writing for Juniors* which focuses particularly on the nine to 11 age-range. The title of the book appears to have been a matter of doubt, for Maybury notes that an alternative could have been 'imaginative writing' although he would have preferred to use the name borrowed from Margaret Langdon, 'intensive writing'. These alternatives all refer to 'encouraging children to use fully what they have within themselves: ideas, impressions, feelings, fears, hopes, their imagination and such language as they can command' (Maybury, 1967, p. 10).

A central feature of Maybury's approach is, like Pym's, 'sense training', although the starting points share the approach of Langdon and Cooper in the use of poetry, and also include music and walks outside the school. Maybury goes beyond these other writers in his concern for drawing out various items of vocabulary and compiling blackboard lists. He provides a compendium of starting points mixed with anthologies of children's writing on the 'direct stimulus' of fire, water, space, things, sound and pictures, and the themes of weather, activities and play, animals, the supernatural, places, people and seasonal topics. There are additional chapters on story writing and various 'techniques' for making special effects with words. Overall the structure of the book moves from the personal experience of the child outward to the wider world.

Lane and Kemp's (1967) *An Approach to Creative Writing in the Primary School* takes a similar perspective, although it includes photographs of stimuli and of children's writing to illustrate what could come from the kind of approach which they propose. There is no clear definition of how 'creative writing' differs from other kinds, but the preface makes it clear that the authors share Maybury's concern for seeking ways of effectively stimulating children to create verbal images.

> The purpose of this book is to try to help those who find it difficult to provide stimuli for talking and writing, and to give them some guidance

on the 'feeding in' of new experience to the child. We must recognise that children write most readily in response to stimuli which 'evoke an image' (Lane and Kemp, 1967, p. v).

Considering the whole primary age-range, Lane and Kemp also begin with the senses and provide additional chapters on the use of music and the use of pictures. Other themes for selecting starting points are covered, such as traditional rhymes and stories, literature and scripture and the environment. There are also chapters on diary work, the comic strip, and writing for a magazine. The attention to diary work may seem a departure from the stimulus-response emphasis of the other creative writing books, but in fact teacher direction is seen as playing a big part even here. From the 'news' tradition of the infant stage, there are suggestions for the teacher of the first year junior class to encourage writing of 'imaginative diaries', including extremely contrived and demanding ones: 'the diary of the classroom hamster' for Year 1, or, to link in with work in history, 'the diary of a prisoner in a dungeon, awaiting execution', for Year 2.

The title of Noel Holmes' (1967) *The Golden Age for English* refers to the possibilities of the junior age range, when freed from the constraints of the 11+ examinations, being able to build upon the strengths of seven- to 11-year-olds 'for limitless curiosity, enthusiasm and discovery; and for the development of previously acquired skills' (Holmes, 1967, p. vii). There is no doubt about the assumed need for 'vividness' in these children's responses to the teacher's stimuli for writing. 'By "creative writing" is meant employing words as children use paints, when, with blue, vermilion and burnt sienna, they produce a sunset' (Holmes, 1967, p. 3). Holmes' examples of children's writing include similar starting points to the other books: titles, ideas, opening sentences, music, paintings and photographs, shapes and objects. There is a chapter on 'Junior School Journalism' although the magazine and newsboard seemed to have been used as a means of collating the writing which resulted from the starting points, rather than for generating a particular type of 'journalistic' writing in itself. Where Holmes does move in a different direction from earlier publications is in the detail of his chapter on verse in which the nature and possibilities of the teaching of more 'classical' verse forms as well as free verse are outlined.

Haggitt's (1967) *Working with Language* provides a more direct use of literature for encouraging junior school children's writing, particularly of novels. The approach offered here includes the rewriting and reworking of plots and themes of major stories such as the Odyssey, and works by Hemingway, Steinbeck, Garner and Tolkien. Haggitt also distinguishes between writing from indirect and direct experience and using precise language. Creative writing is referred to again and Haggitt reports encouraging children to use similes and add 'colour' to their writing, which he sees as being the most formative part of language experience. On a summer's day, he reports,

I had asked the class to lie face downwards on the grass and to write in their rough books what they felt and what they saw. The children were told to look for 'poetic' moments . . . (Haggitt, 1967, p. 64).

A chapter on music, movement and drama is also used to show that these experiences can also create an atmosphere conducive to 'virile' language expression. At the same time Haggitt argues that there is definitely a place for precise or 'business-like' language in schools, writing in which children 'state facts precisely and without ambiguity' (p. 90), although he quickly adds that in his school 'we do not disregard the opportunities for "creative" writing in such work'.

The final book of the same year was Marie Peel's (1967) *Seeing to the Heart*, again concentrating on the junior school years. The title is taken from the work of Ruskin and refers to the essence of the 'imagination', which Peel discusses in great depth in relation to its potential in realising a pupil's 'creative individuality'. The book has the most detailed discussion of any so far mentioned and is distinguished by a very thoughtful consideration of the subtle relationships between children's imagination and experience and the context of their work in schools. Although the underlying framework is basically concerned with 'creative writing' and the planning of appropriate 'stimuli', the index of the book has references for creative writing only to the chapters on writing but not to the one on projects or to the section on letter writing in the chapter on language. Furthermore, Peel (1967, p. 143) distinguishes between objective (or factual) writing and 'personal writing', although it is not made fully clear how these relate to 'creative writing'.

Within a few years, this kind of finer differentiation was taken up by a further wave of publications, which represented a range of responses to the notion of creative writing. Some authors were prepared to stay with the possibilities of stimulating children to experiment with the forms of written language, without going on to discuss other kinds of writing, because of a narrow preoccupation with 'English', rather than with writing throughout the curriculum (for example Gregson, 1973). Other authors were apparently using the term synonymously with virtually any kind of writing: writing to a friend, describing a new hat, reporting an event, expressing our views about pay negotiations, telling a story about an experience. 'Each of these represents a form of creative writing' (Yardley, 1970, p. 113).

A different view is taken by Roberts (1972), in *English in Primary Schools*, who cautions against any assumption that stimulating children in 'creative writing' and follow-up help in spelling and punctuation is 'all that can be done' to improve children's writing. He suggests that it is necessary to encourage a cycle of motivation, precise learning, improvement and application of any newly-learned skills. Rather than dwell on 'creative writing' Roberts prefers to distinguish between descriptive and imaginative writing, although it is not clear how this distinction relates to the earlier advice to young teachers to classify children's writing into story telling, informative writing and evaluative writing in order to study the different demands that they make upon the young writer. Roberts' main distinction, though, is between writing which is divergent and based on the child's notions of a theme (imaginative) and that which delineates a field (descriptive).

Peter Armitstead's (1972) *English in the Middle Years* distinguishes between a number of kinds of writing: notes to record items, resolving problems, writing out of personal issues, factual, playing with language, using literary forms. There is an uneasy passing reference to 'creative' writing in the personal issues section and, as in other publications, a good deal on 'stimuli' (content, feeling, language and form), but unlike the others rather more on the different senses of 'audience' in the various kinds of writing outlined. Others, however, were beginning to show some direct reservations about creative writing. Tucker's (1973) *Teaching English in the Middle Years* expresses misgivings about the creative writing lesson which involves a fragmenting of language work, perhaps being hived off to a student teacher, while the class teacher continues with the task of real 'English', perhaps in the form of exercises.

> Serving teachers have now grown used to students who light small fires on their desks and who play records of 'Fingal's Cave' . . . (Tucker, 1973, p. 29).

As a way out of this overemphasis and to try to break away from this narrow conception of writing types, Tucker adopts a division made in a 1968 newsletter from an Edinburgh Reading Centre by W. S. Jackson: personal, imaginative and impersonal. Personal writing involves writing on experiences, reactions or an awareness of situations, which may be contrived by the teacher or spontaneous. There may be only a vague boundary between this kind of writing and children's imaginative writing about experiences in which they have not necessarily participated. Impersonal writing is 'functional writing', setting down facts objectively.

Sybil Marshall's (1974) *Creative Writing* also includes reservations about the creative writing approach but remains fundamentally committed to it without systematically relating it to other kinds of writing. Marshall's definition of creative writing owes much to Suzanne Langer:

> . . . the use of written language to conceptualise, explore and record experience in such a way as to create a unique symbolisation of it (Marshall, 1974, p. 10).

Marshall is aware of the excesses which can creep into such teaching and examines four variations of interpretation put upon the term which might lead to a degeneration in quality. One is the move to extremes of free writing which, she argues, may still need the teacher's support in the sorting and ordering of thoughts and some advice on presentation. A second is the concern for the revelation of the child's 'inner self' which might be expressed by emotional reactions to sensory stimulation ('the burning of joss sticks in an inner room'). This aspect of creative writing teaching can get out of proportion and fail to allow for the fact that children select and assimilate experience in their own individual way. To try to 'involve' them may in fact do nothing more than confront them with what seem to children to be unimportant phenomena, unworthy of the expense of emotion. The 'flowing style' beloved of creative writing teachers represents a further weakness in the interpretation of the approach. The cramming in of adjectives and adverbs can produce writing which may be 'creative', in her definition, but which may also 'slip away into crazy convolutions' (Marshall, 1974, p. 16). Finally, a misinterpretation has centred on the belief that only so-called 'poetry' can really be creative. There is a 'razor's edge' for the teacher to negotiate here. Free verse (subtly chosen sentences and phrases 'listed' on a page) may not be any more 'creative' than prose, although, Marshall argues, the former may well be the best means of children developing creative writing. Paradoxically, sophisticated awareness of the possibilities of language in free verse forms may come principally from experience of more formal and traditional verse forms. Yet it may be unwise to over-encourage children to attempt to write such forms because of 'dreadful things' which children can produce in attempting rhyme and scansion.

A year earlier, however, there had been a more fundamental criticism of the general creative writing movement. Ashworth's (1973) *Language in the Junior School* includes a searching examination of the nature of and claims for 'creative writing'. Ashworth accepts that it has liberated teachers from the previous overemphasis on the conventions of syntax and the 'correctness' of writing, as well as widening the subject matter to include literary or sensory experiences and the forms in which the subject matter could be represented. On the other hand, Ashworth takes issue with the claims of Clegg (1964) and others that involvement in creative writing will lead to an improvement in all kinds of writing and also have a certain therapeutic value. He points out the therapeutic possibilities of other kinds of writing and even more so of other kinds of language, particularly speech. To counter this danger of the exclusivist tendency of the creative writing movement, he reiterates that one of the principal features of the whole of human language competence is its creative nature. He reminds us of Chomsky's work revealing the 'generative competence' of human language, the ability to continually create new, yet intelligible sentences; and the work of Hymes and Halliday in highlighting 'communicative competence', which illustrates the creative use of language strategies in adjusting to various circumstances.

To categorise writing 'types', Ashworth seems to settle for the ideas of Britton which had been published in 1970 and which had formed the basic conceptual framework in Jones and Mulford's (1971) *Children Using Language*. Misgivings on the teaching of 'creative writing' were already apparent here. After the description of an 'object lesson' by Connie Rosen, the editors add:

> The children in Connie Rosen's class talked and wrote about their experiences: they did not set out at any time to do 'creative writing'. The

issue of making creative writing a special (sometimes time-tabled) activity will be taken up at several places in this book (Jones and Mulford, 1971, p. 26).

This book is the outcome of the work of the Primary Schools Sub-Committee of the National Association for the Teaching of English (NATE). As such, it represents a slight shift in thinking from that indicated in this association's journal two years earlier (NATE, 1969), which has contributions by teachers on creative writing, although the editorial draws attention to other articles which take a 'cool look' at creative writing.

The model of language functions put forward by Britton was to come to dominate thinking about children's writing just as much as the notion of creative writing did a decade earlier. Before dealing with it, though, it is worth having a critical look back over developments in thinking since 1950 in the books which have been considered.

One can sense a general growth in awareness in the ways in which teachers had approached their work on children's writing. Although several of the books deal with the junior age-range only, this growth in awareness had permeated the whole of the primary age-range. Even by the early 'sixties the Chief Inspector of Primary Schools was to say 'the single most dramatic change for the better in Primary education since the war has been in written work . . . this change is seen in its most surprising manifestations in the upper Infants' classes . . .' (Blackie, 1963, p. 36). Certainly a striking feature of these books is the wealth of teaching experience reflected in the range of practical ideas and examples of children's work. Most teachers may prefer to exploit their relative autonomy in British schools and plan their curriculum according to their general circumstances and those of their children. At the same time, many will wish to dip into various books for ideas and examples to act as catalysts for forward planning or as elements to fit into established plans. In this respect each book will be seen to have its own strengths: perhaps Lane and Kemp for work on the senses, Holmes for musical sources, Haggitt for the use of stories, Maybury for the development of themes and Clegg for using the local environment, even in its most industrialised form.

But these and the other publications also illustrate the lack of an agreed framework of writing types for work with the primary school age-range. A whole battery of labels have been bandied about – personal, creative, informative, imaginative, business-like, intensive, impersonal – without the overlaps and ambiguities being properly clarified. Ironically the author who is most often quoted by others, Margaret Langdon, did not see her category of intensive writing used in further volumes. Of course the lack of any systematic research makes it very difficult to estimate how far the concerns of these authors have been those of the primary school teachers of the last forty years or so. Despite this reservation, though, it does appear likely that 'creative writing' enjoyed a boom in primary schools in the 'sixties and 'seventies, even if its origins could have been in a Bristol PGCE course.

Quite why this boom occurred is possibly due to several factors. The phasing out of the selection examinations at 11+ gave teachers a great deal more opportunity to experiment with teaching methods. The fact that 'English' was more open-ended than other 'basic' subjects such as mathematics, provided a ready-made area for innovation. The possibilities for creative writing work generating vivid vocabulary items would have appealed, as the use of new and unusual words has probably always been an important index of writing development for many teachers (DES, 1982a). The situation also allowed enthusiastic teachers or student teachers to be able quickly to make an impact in a classroom in a key curriculum area by the use of various stimuli or starting points. As the children dutifully responded with more and more adjectives, adverbs, similes and metaphors, it is easy to see how the extremes crept in. (Marshall reports children being asked to base their writing on their handling of a dead herring in a darkened room.)

Moreover, as Mulford (1969) says, the stimulus-response model of Pym and Langdon can be seen as an interim stage in the reaction against the aridity of the past. In the heady years of the creative writing boom, the ideas of some of the more sensitive writers, for example Cutforth, may have been relatively neglected, ideas such as allowing writing to grow naturally out of environmental studies or be an integral part of the newsroom approach of newspapers, quizzes and arguments. In fact, for some creative writing may well have become an almost exclusive concern in this area of language work, as Ashworth feared. Haggitt's book, for example, seems very reluctant to encourage other types of writing in factual work, because he singles out Holmes' magazines and Lane and Kemp's diary work as further avenues for teacher-stimulated writing.

These kinds of tendencies also meant that Gagg's interesting notion of 'study writing' was never followed up in other publications. The writing up of a simple scientific experiment or a summary of what a child had learned about the history of a local castle rarely featured in discussions or anthologies. Certainly there was little sign of a sharing of teaching possibilities such as those featured in Lane and Kemp, Maybury, or Tucker, despite their eschewal of the narrower subject view of English taken by Gregson. There was even less sign of children being encouraged or helped to develop a sustained argument of any kind, contributing to the pedagogical vacuum in this aspect of writing noted later by Her Majesty's Inspectors (DES, 1978).

Perhaps an even more fundamental weakness is the lack of some of the main features of a conceptual model of the writing process adopted in this book, such as aim and audience. As suggested earlier, the production of written language often lacks the support of the conversational partner who is normally present in spoken language and generally involves a more distant and perhaps less well-defined audience. Thus to make school writing as psychologically realistic as possible, aim and audience need to be given as much attention as is appropriate for the age and ability of the children. In this way, an increasingly differentiated model of writing types could be accommodated. It could also be encapsulated by a terminology which indicated the different possible growth points within the writing process, such as an increased awareness of possible adjustments for aim, audience, content and mode.

Successive publications by the DES have drawn attention to such issues. Back in 1931 the report of the Hadow Committee, *The Primary School*, suggested that older junior children's writing should range over several writing types, narrative, description and some exposition and argumentation, although 'purposes' for writing were not properly considered (Harpin, 1976, p. 26). A handbook of suggestions published after the second world war warned against the fragmentation of English teaching and encouraged teachers to help children develop the 'craft' of writing and plan beyond a 'shapeless transcription of memories and impressions' (Ministry of Education, 1954, p. 63). More suggestions five years later (DES, 1959) again stressed the use of first-hand experience, reasons for writing, respect for the reader and a purposeful but not over-anxious approach to accuracy. The Plowden Report (DES, 1967, p. 219) gave an unqualified welcome to the 'rather grandly named' creative writing where children could communicate something which had 'really engaged' minds and imaginations. A subsequent survey of 20 schools reported seeing a mix of pedestrian and lively creative writing in part of a section on 'personal writing'. This was in turn distinguished from 'informative' writing reported as the kind most commonly seen (DES, 1970). By 1975, the Bullock Committee (DES, 1975, p. 163) reported a 'healthy scepticism' about the value of creative writing, especially when pumped up by the teacher and divorced from real feeling. The primary school survey (DES, 1978) did not witness as much creative writing of this kind as had been expected and went as far as to applaud its absence (DES, 1978, p. 49).

TWO CURRENT ALTERNATIVE FRAMEWORKS: BRITTON AND KINNEAVY

Therefore by the early 1970s there was some disillusionment with creative writing and an underlying recognition of the need for a broader framework which embraced the possibilities of genuine personal expression and growth through writing, the construction of the poetic forms beloved of the creative writing movement, and which also included the kinds of writing involved in more information-based curriculum areas and which sometimes demanded that pupils explicitly argue a point of view. Two such frameworks will be considered here, both of which can be represented diagrammatically. Both allow a classification related to the writer's intention, in contrast to the largely mode or form-based concerns of many of the publications reviewed earlier in this chapter. Both have particular features to commend them and offer much to teachers involved in attempting to develop a well-founded differentiation in children's writing.

Britton

The more widely known of the two is Britton's model of language functions, which owes its origins to Sapir, Harding, Langer, Moffett and others. Three main functions are proposed, one of which is sub-divided:

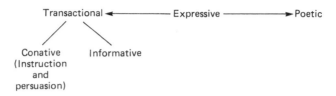

The central dimension is a continuum along which any writing can be 'placed'. The central category is the 'expressive' one, talking or writing which verbalises the inner consciousness, assumes a close relationship with listener or reader and which is relatively unstructured, evidenced especially in everyday 'gossip' and diaries. From here, the continuum moves outwards to poetic language where the writing can be admired for its form, as in stories, poetry, plays and songs, and to transactional language which is the language of getting things done, such as in records, reports, essays, letters of complaint.

Poetic language results from taking up the role of 'spectator' on the world; transactional from taking up the role of 'participant'. There are additional sub-categories in the model which can be seen in full in a Schools Council Research Study *The Development of Writing Abilities (11–18)* (Britton, 1975) and complete, except for the additional sub-categories, in a journal paper 'What's the Use?' (Britton, 1971). The problem of 'dual function' writing, such as a poem deliberately written to effect action, can be dealt with by additional bracketed items – for example, poetic (persuasive). There is also an additional category, 'other', for language activities such as 'dummy run' English exercises, which fail to take up the proper demands of the task they seek to 'demonstrate'.

These categories have much in common with the three major models of English teaching in secondary schools identified by Dixon (1975): models which concentrate on skills, personal growth and the cultural heritage of poetry and prose. The skills model may have been more akin to the dummy-run additional category, but clearly it has a potential affinity with the transactional skills of the informative and conative functions. By classifying the functions of writing in this way, the attempts to improve children's 'skills' of accuracy and appropriateness might be better served.

Britton also outlines a framework of audience categories (see opposite).

Britton's category system was developed as part of the Schools Council research into the development of writing abilities in secondary schools but has also been convincingly adopted in several books on the primary age-range (Jones and Mulford, 1971; West Sussex County Council, 1976;

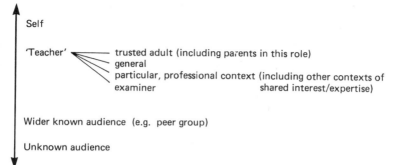

Mallett and Newsome, 1977; Hutchcroft *et al.*, 1981). It was also the principal theoretical framework for the parts on writing in the Bullock Report (DES, 1975). The collection by Jones and Mulford contains an especially distinguished paper by Nancy Martin entitled 'What are they up to?', a discussion of a week's output from three classes, aged seven, nine and 11, which would repay study by anyone interested in following through an application of Britton's ideas to younger children's language use.

Despite or perhaps because of its new orthodoxy, Britton's work has been subjected to criticism, some of it surprisingly vitriolic. The relevance of such debates to primary school teachers is partially restricted by their focus on the teaching of English in secondary schools. One source of criticism is Whitehead's sardonically titled 'What's the Use, Indeed?' (1978) which shows that Whitehead is unhappy at Britton's preoccupation with categorising and with the implications of the expressive–poetic relationship in the model, where gossip can be linked in a continuity with literature, in a way which may exalt the significance of the former and denigrate the distinctive qualities of the latter.

The unhappiness with the apparent centrality of 'gossip' in Britton's perspectives on English teaching is shared by Allen (1980). He suggests that the transactional–expressive continuum is of no help in making decisions about the quality and maturity of writing and thus undervalues literature in promoting growth in English.

The most aggressive attack on Britton's work and the research project of which he was director, has come from Williams (1977). Her attack is centred on the lack of rigour in the methodology behind the research which Britton directed and the inconsistency in its philosophical assumptions. On the model of language functions itself, Williams is concerned at the impression given by the definition of 'expressive' and wonders whether it justifies a separate category. She also questions whether expressive writing is necessarily similar to expressive speech, which Britton seems to assume, as it does not share its 'involuntariness'. Overall, Williams is wary of an attempt to generate a theory of language which embraces both English teaching and other subjects because she sees teachers of the latter being principally concerned with language as a means rather than as an integral part of their subject matter.

In a detailed reply to Williams' criticisms, Britton (1979) is notably concerned to defend the notion of 'expressive' language and charts its origins from the earlier part of the century. He reaffirms that expressive writing is that which presupposes an interest in the writer as well as in what the writer has to say about the world. It can be usefully distinguished from 'externalised' and 'decontextualised' communications of information (transactional language) or a work of art in language (poetic language) and it can play a recurrent role in the assimilation of new knowledge to an individual's existing knowledge through talk and writing throughout the school years and beyond.

Kinneavy

The most integrated model of language types categorised by aim is that of Kinneavy (1971), although it is probably far less well known than Britton's work. Kinneavy makes it clear in the preface of his book that his framework represents an attempt to present a coherent and unified view of the field of English which has some measure of internal consistency. Kinneavy takes as his basic structure the nature of the language process itself, as represented in the so-called communication triangle, the origins of which can be traced back to Aristotle's study of rhetoric. Applied to writing, the triangle can be constructed as follows:

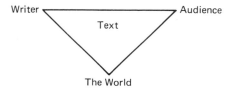

Kinneavy shows how abstractions from the triangle can be made to establish three basic areas of study in English, syntactics, semantics and pragmatics (the study of discourse). In applying the triangle to the latter, he highlights how four basic 'aims' of discourse can be related to the stress of the language process, being on either the producer, the audience, the product or the reality of the world to which it refers. These different aims are shown in the diagram opposite (above).

The stress on expressive aims is on language being used as the simple vehicle of expression or some aspect of the personality of the writer (or speaker). If the focus is on the audience, the aims are persuasive, trying to encourage change in behaviour or belief. Referential aims involve the stress being on the ability of language to designate or 'reproduce' the reality of the world. Kinneavy prefers referential to 'expository', as the latter does not distinguish what is said from why it is said. Finally, literary aims concen-

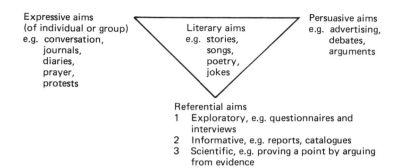

Expressive aims
(of individual or group)
e.g. conversation,
    journals,
    diaries,
    prayer,
    protests

Literary aims
e.g. stories,
    songs,
    poetry,
    jokes

Persuasive aims
e.g. advertising,
    debates,
    arguments

Referential aims
1   Exploratory, e.g. questionnaires and
    interviews
2   Informative, e.g. reports, catalogues
3   Scientific, e.g. proving a point by arguing
    from evidence

trate on the text itself as an object capable of being appreciated in its own right.

The modes of discourse are set out by Kinneavy as alternative ways of referring to 'reality', by narrative, classification, evaluation or description. To each of these four, he suggests, there corresponds a principle of thought which permits reality to be considered in a particular way in discourse, with a particular logic, organisational pattern and style.

As with the framework of Britton, there have been criticisms. A central one made by Odell *et al.*, (1978) is that Kinneavy's is a theory of discourse products, not language processes and therefore it may be of limited value in work on helping improve the composing of writing. They also warn of the difficulties of categorising writing in this way, especially where aims are unclear or where pieces which are categorised similarly feel 'intuitively' different. Lloyd-Jones (1977) further adds a note of caution on how 'pure' motives for writing can be: we write for many reasons.

Nevertheless, theoretical frameworks like those of Britton and Kinneavy can be useful in making us aware of the basic purposes for which written language can be used. Each makes distinctions between the producer of the language, the audience for it, the message and the world to which it refers.

There are possibilities for using such models as the basis for future research into the ways in which various features of writing development can be fostered by involvement in different types. Like Ashworth earlier, Odell *et al.* (1978) also warn that skill in fulfilling one kind of aim in writing does not necessarily imply skill in accomplishing another: the writer of a good technical report may not be able to produce an excellent persuasive letter (Lloyd-Jones, 1977, p. 37). Some steps towards ways of formulating this kind of two dimensional research model have been taken by Wilkinson *et al.* (1980), discussed earlier, and Bereiter (1980), who notes the areas of overlap between his own stages and the categories of Britton. How far it is helpful to plan curriculum activities in ways which will encourage and allow pupils to use writing in these different ways is obviously still a matter for debate. In the book based on her Schools Council project 'Language Development in the Primary School', Connie Rosen reports how many teachers have a home-made set of categories of written language which they more or less work to. Yet, she adds, these categories tend to be based on mature adult discourse and tell us nothing of how children learn to handle different varieties of language.

This is true, but Mrs Rosen's next point is perhaps more questionable: she suggests that categories based on adult discourse do not provide us with a system for looking at primary school children's 'immature' kinds of writing, whereas earlier in her book she gives an indication of this kind of 'diagnostic' application of such categories.

> . . . do we need writing to live and act together in the way that we need talk? There are kinds of writing which clearly fulfil these functions – many personal letters, the controversies which fill newspapers and books, and all kinds of written information from labels on bottles to encyclopedias. Very little of what children write is of this instrumental kind, though they sometimes have things to say to their teacher and to other children which is genuinely informative. Perhaps more contact with people and life outside school would give rise to more of this (Rosen and Rosen, 1973, p. 142).

It is axiomatic that teachers work towards encouraging growth in children's writing through differentiation of aims and modes and in helping them to adjust to different senses of audience across a considerable range of content. It is clearly good for children that this should be the case. How far children's own interests can be incorporated into teachers' work, through the encouragement of personal writing, is not so clear. Similarly, writing in response to creative writing stimuli may do little more than to increase children's sensitivity to sensory experiences or to raise their awareness of the metaphorical possibilities of their language. From an overall perspective, therefore, it seems safer to try to ensure a balanced differentiation, through adopting a framework which is effectively related to the writing process and its situational context and which carries with it clear implications as to how the teacher may best intervene to promote growth. It is with these kinds of issues in mind that the following chapters have been planned. Chapter 7 outlines the possible contexts of primary school children's writing and, like chapter 8, discusses selections of their writing within Kinneavy's clearly structured framework. Chapter 9 suggests how teachers' interventions to develop various component skills in children's writing might be especially fruitful. First, though, we need to look at how children begin to write.

6 The beginnings of writing

Any account of the ways in which children may develop early writing skills needs to pay careful attention to what kinds of background and expectations children bring to the task.

A small piece of recent research confirms many earlier findings on the relative importance of the home. Raban (1982) has studied a small sample of children from the Bristol longitudinal language development project of Wells (1981a) reported earlier (see chapter 3). She reports that positive home influences (indicated by transcripts, and interviews with parents from the pre-school years) are significantly related to the quality of children's writing at five, seven and nine, whereas the influence of the school was only positively associated with writing quality in children from 'poor' homes, as defined in the study. Material on 'antecedents' of children's writing attainment from the Bristol study has been further discussed by Kroll in Kroll and Wells (1983).

Of course, if children's expectations of writing are considered, then their expectations of reading must be also, as the two skills are normally introduced close together. In a curious way, there appear to be similarities and differences between children's expectations of writing and reading. For many young children the abstract nature of written language in general is a source of doubt and uncertainty. The nature and importance of reading and writing activities are not clear to them. Downing (1969), argues that to avoid this 'cognitive confusion' it is important to involve children in learning experiences in which they can appreciate the real purposes of reading and writing. Activities such as talking about recipes and instructions will also strengthen their understanding of the technical concepts of language, such as 'words' and 'letters'.

At the same time, there may well be differences between children's expectations of the two activities. Children may often seem to attempt writing more naturally than reading, presumably because the end result is more directly observable and writing is easier to imitate than silent reading. Perhaps even more importantly, the making of written symbols may be in itself a deeply satisfying act for many children.

As Ajuriaguerra and Auzias (1975, p. 312) put it, 'The hand that speaks gives pleasure to the child, for whom it is a "discovery" and a means of representing something within himself'. Britton (1972) reports a three-year-old child making a six-page book of 'mock writing' in the form of saw-tooth lines. Graves (1978b) goes so far as to suggest that a child's first urge is to write rather than to read and that this can assist early reading in the way in which it 'makes' reading and brings into use the auditory, visual and kinaesthetic skills which contribute to it. Wells (1981b, p. 274) is similarly convinced that waiting for children to become quite fluent readers before encouraging them to compose written texts is to miss many opportunities to become aware of the power and limitations of written language. Where weaknesses in handwriting skills exclude such possibilities, 'writing aloud' by dictating to an adult, or to a tape-recorder, and the use of some kind of device like the sentence-maker in the *Breakthrough to Literacy* materials (Mackay, 1980) might be used.

Whether or not such predispositions to write do appear, there are certain skills and insights which can be usefully developed in children for later use in writing, more specifically manual dexterity and language facility. These broad areas of skill and facility can be seen as the foundations of a constellation of other skills discussed earlier in chapter 3. If these skills and insights are encouraged within a purposeful context for reading and writing suggested by Downing, then the foundations for the growth of early writing skills can be laid down in a number of useful ways.

However, whatever is done to help development of manual dexterity needs to be continually related to the general experiences of books, talk and family life. Therefore three important considerations for parents and those involved in running playgroups and nursery classes are:

- making full use of opportunities for talking with children and sharing books with them;

- involving children in activities which develop large motor skills;

- channelling children's scribbles into helpful pre-writing patterns.

USING OPPORTUNITIES FOR TALKING AND SHARING BOOKS

Before embarking on any consideration of ideas on the long-term development of children's writing, it is important to re-emphasise the fundamental relationships between writing and other uses of language. Although it may be difficult to pin-point the exact nature of the influence of children's oral language development on later writing abilities, it seems both wise and appropriate that any attempts to develop children's writing should co-exist with an awareness of the value of talking things over with children, particularly the kind of talk which builds upon the 'here and now' and links it to the past and the future, to imagination, speculation and generalisation. A number of conceptual frameworks for this kind of work now exist, including the compensatory approaches of the Gahagans (1970), ways of meeting the cognitive demands of the school (Tough, 1977), and the implications of the naturalistic studies of Wells (1981b).

Similarly, the continual sharing of books with children will provide a growing store of experience. Such experience has been shown to be significantly linked to awareness of the purposes and mechanics of literacy and later school attainment (Wells, 1981a). It also provides children with a 'linguistic resource' in the knowledge of the ways in which stories and other modes of discourse are structured and presented. Most fundamentally of all, perhaps, the steady growth of children's literacy skills will be even more likely if they are cared for in circumstances which offer security and support by others who in turn respect the uniqueness of every child's personality and experience of life.

DEVELOPING LARGE MOTOR SKILLS AND PRE-WRITING PATTERNS

The necessary motor skills will come initially from those which seem to have little direct relation to writing – gross motor skills involved in making simple collages, junk models and a whole range of sorting, cutting, pasting, painting and making activities. From here, children can be encouraged to adapt their scribbles and doodles in ways which are closer to written language forms. In an outstanding book written for parents, Mackay and Simo (1976) set out suggestions for simple repetitive patterns which use movements similar to those used in making many letters:

rain   pin men   S snakes   bridges   ∴ dots   ⌒ curves

zigzags   waves   spirals   ○ suns   × kisses

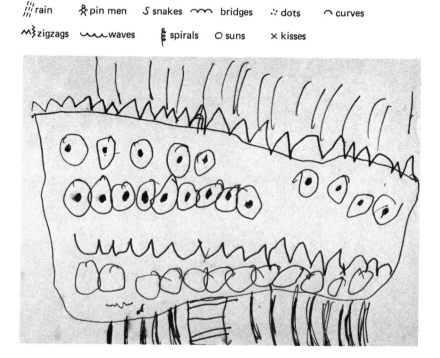

See how Hannah (4) has incorporated some of these into a picture. Such patterns may be best tackled first with larger drawing implements, wax crayons or chalk, for instance, before the finer motor skill of pencil use is applied to these kinds of letter shapes, and the correct grip of the pencil is checked and practised.

LANGUAGE FACILITY

Another vital area of pre-writing development is in the uses of spoken language which are likely to be most helpful in the writing context. King and Rentel (1979) suggest that these can be identified as unsupported utterances, the application of internalised story structures and the ability to control the interplay between the various aspects of the unsupported utterances, such as situation, audience and intentions. Therefore it seems that parents and teachers should:

- encourage the development of children's unsupported utterances;
- allow children to apply their knowledge of story structures;
- help children experience the interplay between such aspects of writing as situation, audience and intentions.

Unsupported utterances

The third of the uses listed above will be dealt with later in the book, but in turning briefly to the first, it is clear that adults need to become good listeners. This quality is vital for those who spend time with young children in playgroups and nurseries as well as in homes and schools. The production of 'unsupported utterances' is a major feature of any shift from speech to writing, as was mentioned in the earlier discussion (chapter 3) of Bereiter and Scardamalia's (1982) research into the composing process. Moffett (1968) sums up the change thus:

the first step towards writing is made when a speaker takes over a conversation and sustains some subject alone . . . less collaborative, less prompted, and less corrected by feedback than dialogue.

We can see such a step in this transcript of Gary's (5) contribution to a newstime at the beginning of a school day, with the whole class listening intently. Tape-recording children in this way provides not only a basis for written accounts but also a 'resource for listening' which other children can request at a later time, and around which the teacher can promote more open-ended language use.

Mummy said 'Go to sleep boys' and then my brother he pushed me off the seat and I slept on the floor and then when I woke up, I sat up and didn't know I was on the floor and then I got up off the floor and sat back on the seat and then in about a few minutes time we got to Southampton at the ferry where we went on the ferry and we got on the ferry and when we went up the stairs, my mum didn't know where I was going because there were two sets of stairs one that side and the other that side and my mum said 'What are you doing?' and then when she went down to get some food she went down that side and we went down that side and she did not know where I had gone and when my mummy was going around there, Mummy said 'Where's Gary gone?' and I went back upstairs to Daddy and then when the boat was just starting to go and my mum didn't see all those Navy boats we saw and then when we went out of the dock in about three minutes we got into the dock of the, um, Isle of Wight and then when we got off the ferry there we had to drive from East Cowes dock where we were and then we had to drive right the way down to Sandown and then when we got to Sandown my mum said 'Shall we go down on to the beach?' and I said 'Yes' and when I went into the water we made two friends with two boys when we went into the town and then when we went down to the sea we forced our mum and dad to go on the side where they were so as we could play with them . . .

Applying knowledge of story structures

The second of the language facility uses which seems important for later writing performance is to allow children to develop and use a knowledge of story structures. Recent work on the structure of children's stories suggests that there are various 'story grammars' of which children can become aware by having stories read to them – perhaps some stories many times, if requested. These experiences provide them with insights into typicalities such as formal beginnings and endings, the use of a central character, events which share the same space or time sequence, the use of the past tense, and quotations of speech.

Notice nearly all the above features of narrative structure, except quotations of speech, in Julia's (9) story overleaf.

As was mentioned in chapter 3, Applebee (1978) provides a great deal of insight into how children respond to and use the structure of stories and lends support to those who suggest that the narrative mode plays a central role in the shaping of children's experiences, appearing in pre-sleep monologues around the age of two-and-a-half.

Cowie (1984) has recently brought together a collection of papers on children's imaginative writing which contains a very helpful paper by Kroll and Anson on the structures in children's fictional narratives and which again draws on data from the Bristol longitudinal study referred to in chapter 3 and at the beginning of the chapter.

The old man and the birds

Every day an old man would go down by the river side. He would always take a bag of food and he would feed the birds. The ~~man~~ birds were used to the old man and had grown quite tamed. Some people who passed by him would say look at that silly old man feeding those birds. The old man would sigh those people he thought are unkind. How would they like it if they were birds and hardly ever ate anything. But he cheered up when other people passed and said. Look at that man feeding those birds what a kind hearted man he is. Every day more and more birds would come and be fed.

Now one day the old man was ill and he was very worried about the birds. He could not go down the river for he felt very poorly. The next door neighbour came in the back door and went up to the old mans bedroom. She asked him if he wanted anything. The old man said I ask you one thing would you take a bag of birds food and go and feed the birds. The old lady laughed alright she said. When the old lady got to where the birds were she found lots of birds lined up on a wall.

STAGES OF EARLY WRITING DEVELOPMENT

Basic stages of early writing as assumed in the organisation of teaching have been set out in a number of books – for example, Taylor (1973) and Hutchcroft (1981). How far these approximate to the growth in children's perceptions of writing is not clear because early writing is a relatively under-researched area (Clay, 1980). For the purposes of this book, it seems best to summarise these main teaching stages and then add some comments on issues which spring from them, such as the ways in which children accommodate themselves to the new demands of writing in sentences, a comfortable style of handwriting and, where it occurs, left-handedness.

From such activities as junk-modelling, scribbling and pre-writing patterns, it is normal to plan for children to develop their early writing skills through stages such as these:

- drawing or making something and then dictating writing to the teacher, perhaps trying to trace over the teacher's caption;
- dictating and copying the teacher's caption;
- independent writing.

Drawing or making and dictating

It is well established practice in schools for teachers to write captions dictated by children about things made, painted or drawn. Children can see writing being produced left to right across the page, other conventions of spacing can be quickly appreciated and the words employed can be used to build up a child's own reading vocabulary. Sometimes children are also encouraged to trace over the writing. This work needs to be carefully supervised to prevent incorrect habits of letter formation being developed.

See overleaf how Nigel's (5) attempt at tracing is so bizarre that the use of tracing for him seems inappropriate.

Dictating and copying a caption

The copying of what the teacher has written is likewise a practice widely found in schools. Again there are risks. Children may reproduce the words which the teacher has written for them but, unless they are carefully observed, no-one can be sure of whether they have established a proper sense of 'directionality' and started writing on the left of the page. For some countries of the world right to left is the norm and children need to learn the conventions of English. Some children may just copy letters in a relatively random order. Small group teaching is the most suitable way to deal with this stage, in which directionality and letter formation can be supervised. Practices vary more on actually teaching the latter because some teachers

have reservations about the wisdom of drilling children so early. There are many ways of making letter formation practice enjoyable, though, through regular activities such as tracing letter shapes in the air, or tactile letters either made by teachers or from commercial sources. If air-writing is used, it is obviously important for teachers' instructions to be given looking back at the children over the shoulder.

Marie Clay's (1975) *What Did I Write?* offers a number of insights into children's early writing, based on the many examples which are included in her book. As well as showing where inappropriate concepts of directionality and other features of written language can develop, she identifies several principles which children seem to adopt and practise spontaneously as they begin to write. Two which teachers might be able to particularly build upon are the recurring principle (repeating letters, words or lines to provide a sense of satisfaction) and the inventory principle in which children seem to take stock of their own learning and make lists of what letters or words they know.

INDEPENDENT WRITING

Children's writing will inevitably become increasingly independent at their own rates and teachers need considerable sensitivity in judging when to encourage children to begin trying to write words from memory and to use classroom resources in composing what they want to write. These resources can include tins of words from a child's basic sight vocabulary, folders of words, or cards of words, alphabetically arranged. Hutchcroft *et al.* (1981) give the useful idea of providing each child with a sheet of card 18cm × 24cm which is ruled into twelve squares on each side. Each square can then be used for the gradual listing of two columns of alphabetically arranged words as needed (words beginning with x, y and z sharing the last square). Charts of common irregular words or those from topics (days of the week, weather, colours, pets, centres of interest) can be pinned to the walls of the room to provide further word bank resources, providing they are printed on a large enough scale. These can be used for further incidental teaching of letter formation and spelling patterns as necessary.

An extract from Christopher's (6) book shows where he began to write independently:

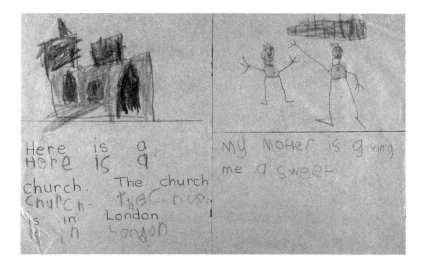

As children become independent writers, word cards may be replaced by simple personal word books, or small alphabetically-arranged sheets stapled together. Particularly at this stage children will benefit from attempting words themselves before checking with teacher. Common patterns of spelling patterns or highly irregular words can form the basis of further group teaching, perhaps part of the overall approach to teaching spelling, dealt with later in this book.

At this stage children might still be struggling with another feature of written language, the sentence. Note for example what Mandy (6) has written:

THE CONCEPT OF A SENTENCE

Kress (1982) suggests that children may face uncertainties in the construction of written sentences. This is because of the fundamental differences in the syntax of speech and writing noted earlier, speech being typically made up of more loosely 'chained' clauses. As they begin to develop their production of written language, children may struggle to produce the discrete syntactical units which make it up. The production of the sentence unit presents a new kind of linguistic challenge, in that the main clause has to be planned for the main idea and any subordinate clauses built around it. According to Kress, children may at first produce textual rather than syntactical units, perhaps using the line of writing as a basis. Kress provides examples of children's writing in which two or three sentences are run together and punctuated as if they were one. Because the constituent 'sentences' are on a common theme, he uses these findings as evidence that children's early concept of a sentence is as a textual rather than a syntactical unit, performing an almost paragraph-like role. He concludes that it is only when a child can actually structure writing in paragraphs that the concept of sentence becomes properly clear, as a 'minimum unit of argument'.

Like Applebee (1978), Kress points out the great help that the use of the narrative mode can give children. In narrative writing the 'events control the writer' in many ways and children are able to develop textual devices which they have established in spoken language, such as the ordering of events in time, the use of the past tense and the use of a setting.

HANDWRITING

The style of handwriting which a child develops can have important ramifications. The ability to translate thoughts into an effective written form depends upon its ease, speed and legibility. Moreover, as will be reported later, swift, well-formed handwriting is highly related to success in spelling (Peters, 1967). Research has indicated that teachers are inclined to award higher credit to writing which is in an agreeable style (Briggs, 1970). Therefore some basic priorities for teachers suggest themselves:

- establish correct letter formation early;
- ensure a consistent school policy in handwriting;
- maintain opportunities for regular practice;
- keep handwriting in a realistic perspective.

Shaughnessy (1977) reminds us of how the handwriting styles of college 'Basic Writing' students are so much 'part of themselves' that they are difficult to change. Inappropriate habits can prove very difficult to modify in later years.

Establish correct letter formation early

Handwriting skill is founded on correct letter formation of which the basic styles are:

Italic style (from Ruth Fagg's *Everyday Writing* Book 5)

The old man turned to throw the thing he held into the fire of spitting birch logs. In that moment Aquila saw what it was.

Round hand style (Marion Richardson's *Writing and Writing Patterns* Book 4)

I had a little nut tree,
Nothing would it bear,
But a silver nutmeg,
And a golden pear.

Modern running or cursive style (from Joyce and Peter Young's *Write and Spell* Book 4)

What could you give away but still keep?

Nearly all small letter shapes are formed without lifting the pencil from the paper, the only exceptions being f, k, t, x and y. The small letters, arranged in 'families' according to basic shape, are normally taught first, a point worth emphasising to parents of pre-school children. Later, capital letters can be taught in three groups and attention can be given to the proportion of letters in relation to each other.

In Great Britain, plain paper is normally used in the early stages although in the USA lined paper is often used from the beginning (Graves, 1978b). For many young children, lines are extremely difficult to conform to when they already have to try to attend to a daunting number of other considerations in the processes of composition and transcription. Lines may be better introduced later when their demands are relatively less of a burden. Plain paper seems to be more appealing for use in special displays, as it allows far greater flexibility in the use of lettering size, layout and illustrations. Ruled guidelines placed under the page can reassure those who are uncertain in the use of plain paper. There are schools where nothing but plain paper is used. (I have to admit a preference for lined paper when at work and used it for drafting this book, although I use plain paper for letters.) Perhaps in the later years of junior and middle schools, the choice can be best left to the children themselves.

Ensure a consistent school policy

It seems only common sense for all schools to have a carefully worked out policy on handwriting. There are several books which are helpful in developing a school policy, such as those by Smith (1977) and Sassoon (1983).

Maintain opportunities for regular handwriting practice

As the Bullock report recommends (DES, 1975, pp. 184–6), there is much to be said for ensuring that regular attention is given to the development of an economical handwriting style throughout the early primary school years. At least twenty or so minutes a week throughout this time will provide a regular and disciplined application of skills and time to apply these to piece of writing of special aesthetic pleasure, such as a poem or short story which a child has recently drafted. This is particularly important when joined handwriting is introduced, often around the age of eight, and when children are encouraged to use pens, perhaps a year or two later. Where necessary, teachers can also use these sessions to encourage practice of frequently joined letters (tr, ea), common clusters (tions, ous, ment) and the experimentation with different possibilities of layout and margins.

Keep handwriting in a realistic perspective

However, it is important to keep the teaching of handwriting in a realistic perspective. It is possible for schools to give a disproportionate priority to the production and display of immaculately written and decorated pieces but which have an unimpressive content, perhaps even perfunctorily copied from books. Graves (1978b) argues that this is to lose sight of the 'toolness' of handwriting, so that handwriting has become the main event, composition the sideshow. The central processes of planning and composing are often messy processes, in which care and neatness will be eschewed. To help children develop ability to produce swift, well-formed handwriting is obviously a highly worthwhile goal, but it also needs to be part of a context which lays greatest stress on the overriding ability to adapt language to whatever needs arise.

Left-handedness

Research suggests that around 10 per cent of children use their left hand when writing, slightly more boys than girls. This may represent only a fraction of those who have left-handed tendencies. There has been a greater tolerance of left-handedness in recent years and consequently fewer children seem to have been encouraged to overcome any natural preference for writing with the left hand. This opposition probably occurred because it was suspected that left-handers were slower, messier, at a general disadvantage in a right-handed world. Relatively little is published on this topic but, in an admirably concise little book, Clark (1974) recommends three simple practices which will help left-handed children to write more comfortably and successfully:

- make sure that left-handed writers position the paper correctly;

- encourage a higher pen or pencil grip which allows the writing to be seen;

- if a pen is used, ensure that the nib is suitable for left handers.

Incorrect positioning of the paper is a source of many children's problems in that they try to write with the left hand top corner of the paper nearer to them, whereas in fact it is the right hand top corner which should be nearer in their case. A 'horizontal' paper position is also incorrect for left-handers, because it leads to a cramped position and uncomfortable, obscured writing. The danger of the hand obscuring the writing can also be avoided if the pen or pencil is gripped an inch or an inch and a half above the point, a grip which also helps to avoid smudging if ink is used. Finally, although most ball-point pens are suitable for left-handed writers, other pens should be fitted with a nib designed for them.

This chapter has attempted to outline some of the main issues involved in the early stages of children's writing. As children gradually become more accomplished in writing, the scope for teachers to help children develop their abilities and performance is very wide, and is closely related to the nature of the writing process and the circumstances which influence it. These considerations are taken up in the next chapter.

7 The classroom context and the writer's aims

The next two chapters attempt to indicate some possible ways in which different types of children's writing can be developed, by presenting a kind of 'annotated anthology'. Specific ways of improving spelling, vocabulary, syntax and so on are dealt with in chapter 9. Chapters 7 and 8 are concerned with different tasks which might be undertaken within a relatively short time, a few days or weeks, and here the contrast of tasks is undertaken by comparing different aims of writing, adapting Kinneavy's model outlined in chapter 5. This model is used here for several reasons. It has a clearly identified theoretical base, the communication triangle, and yet it has a simplicity and coherence which can be of help in curriculum planning. At the same time, it is reconciled with many of the other labels and frameworks brought together in chapter 5, so that the practical examples and ideas which follow can easily be considered within them.

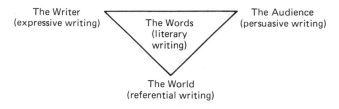

The Writer
(expressive writing)

The Words
(literary
writing)

The Audience
(persuasive writing)

The World
(referential writing)

Before beginning the illustrated exploration of different writing aims, some reference needs to be made to the contexts within which children write in school. These contexts are influenced by such factors as the curriculum experiences which are provided; the teacher's style; and the classroom conditions, such as the use of preparatory talk and whether the subject matter and task are chosen by the children or imposed upon them.

THE CURRICULUM

The context of the curriculum for the primary school years is clearly a major consideration in any appraisal of children's writing in schools. As Harpin (1976, p. 92) reminds us, any assumptions about directions of writing development are incomplete without reference to the experience on which it is based and the audience for whom it is intended. In British schools, there is an extremely wide interpretation of what this experience might be in the 'things that teachers plan that children shall learn and learn to be' (Thomas, 1980, p. 3) which together make up the curriculum.

In recent years there has been something of a reaction against the *laissez-faire* approach towards the primary school curriculum which has been a distinguishing feature of the post-war years. Other than 'basic' skills of language and mathematics, schools vary enormously in their provision in other curriculum areas. For example, the HMI survey of primary schools (DES, 1978) reported that a quarter of the sampled schools undertook no form of history or geography, either as separate subjects or as part of 'topic work'. Granted, thirty-six curriculum items were found to occur individually in at least 80 per cent of the observed classes (for example, discussion of new vocabulary, calculations of four rules, singing), but it needs to be recognised that this list did *not* include such items as drama, spelling, scientific experience, or environmental studies. In fact, on average, only a quarter of all classes were being introduced to all thirty-six items.

The reaction of some commentators on this kind of finding is to question whether such variation in practice is compatible with a genuinely comprehensive educational provision. Richards (1982, p. 48) takes this line in arguing for greater curriculum 'consistency': the introduction of all pupils at a particular stage to a similar set of curriculum elements, whether or not the pupils are in the same class. Richards stresses that he is not arguing for a rigid, centralised control of the curriculum, but instead greater co-ordination, coherence and continuity. In a recent book, he has assembled papers from different commentators which together imply that:

> *laissez-faire* is not just an inappropriate approach to curriculum decision-making but that paradoxically it devalues the professionalism of the individual practitioner by assuming a degree of individual self-sufficiency which could only be sustained if the task in question was simple, uncontentious, fully understood and self-contained. Educating young children is none of these (Richards, 1982, p. 25).

One of the main lines of argument for the *laissez-faire* approach has been that it enables teachers to evolve one of the main innovative features of contemporary primary schools, 'the topic'. Other labels are also used for this feature, such as 'project' or 'centre of interest', but all assume that topic work involves exploring curriculum areas (other than basic reading and number skills) in a thematic way (Kerry, 1982, p. 8). Rance (1968), for instance, lists several common assumptions about topics, including their success in breaking down the artificial barriers that have been erected around the various academic subjects. Yet as many teachers have noted, topic work can produce another kind of fragmentation, the divorce of one topic from the next. Bantock (1980) shares this unease in saying that, by adopting such approaches, the primary school may not effectively 'convey the structures of knowledge in a coherent fashion' resulting in 'a magpie curriculum of bits and pieces, unrelated and ephemeral'. The dangers of topic work becoming superficial and repetitive have been effectively captured in a prize-winning children's novel, *Thunder and Lightnings* (Mark, 1976, pp. 33–7).

Of course, there is no doubt that topic work can be a highly valuable way of helping children become more independent and self-organised learners and indeed many of the skills and attitudes gained are early versions of those needed in work for the long essays and theses of higher education. The possibilities of topic work are similar to those credited to the integrated day by Dearden (1971): it can create situations which resemble anything from an 'embryonic university' to 'a wet play-time all day'.

Recent research in Nottinghamshire (Kerry, 1982) indicates that there is still a considerable amount of uncertainty in teachers' minds about the nature and possibilities of project work. For the purposes of this chapter, though, even if it is agreed that the interrelations between different parts of the curriculum are worth exploring and exploiting, it is still necessary to have some overview of what the curriculum should contain. To this end, it is worth reiterating the curriculum structure adopted by the HMI primary school survey which related skills, ideas and attitudes to the following areas: language and literacy, mathematics, science, aesthetic and physical education, social studies.

There is apparently another advantage in establishing a basic width of curriculum beyond the basic skills of language and mathematics. It seems that children do better in the latter if they are in classes which cover most of the widely taught items in primary schools (DES, 1978, p. 96).

Three cautions must at once be added to this kind of categorising. One is that it should be used in a critical way as a yardstick for positive self-evaluation in schools. There are other equally valid ways of conceptualising the primary school curriculum. The HMI grouping has questionable omissions such as health education and many teachers would prefer physical and aesthetic education to be categorised separately.

Secondly, there is the danger of 'reifying' knowledge, attributing concrete qualities to abstract entities. Arguments which make such assumptions have to be reconciled with views which emphasise the ability of the human mind to organise experience in subjective ways and make interpretations relative to an individual's situation and perspective (Taylor and Richards, 1979, p. 31).

Thirdly, any such analysis should take full cognizance of the multiracial and multicultural nature of modern society. Although some of the linguistic issues which arise from this are touched upon in chapters 3 and 9, the related curriculum issues are examined in some depth in James and Jeffcoate (1981) and Cohen and Manion (1983).

However, this kind of grouping can form a basis, not only for planning learning activities in themselves, but also in a consideration of possible interrelationships between different writing aims and various curriculum areas in promoting the growth of writing abilities, and these have been placed along the third dimension of the model below.

A model such as this may raise more questions than it answers, but the questions which arise can be vital parts of effective curriculum planning

Development of spelling, vocabulary,
syntax, organisation, etc. over time

	Aims of writing			
	EXPRESSIVE	LITERARY	REFERENTIAL exploratory informative scientific	PERSUASIVE
Language and literacy				
Mathematics				
Science				
Aesthetic and physical education (art, craft, movement, music)				
Social studies (geography, history, religious studies)				

(Left axis label: Curriculum areas which can be introduced to foster skills, ideas and attitudes)

and evaluation. In which curriculum areas might expressive writing be best encouraged, other than language and literacy? What kinds of dynamic relationships between language and curriculum experience might evolve from the writing of poetry in religious studies, or scientific accounts of tasks in movement lessons? Which context might best facilitate the development of the subtleties of vocabulary and syntax in the writing of persuasive arguments? These kinds of question underline the fundamental nature of the curriculum framework within which teaching styles will operate and children's experiences be incorporated.

THE TEACHER'S STYLE

Another kind of dynamic relationship which has yet to be researched is the effect of the personal interaction between teachers and pupils on the nature of children's learning. Some steps in this direction have recently been taken by the ORACLE research project (Galton *et al.*, 1980; Galton and Simon, 1980). The findings from this observational research project have to be viewed with some caution in that the sample of schools was relatively small (58 classrooms in 19 schools); measures of attainment were narrowly conceived, principally individual raw scores from modified versions of the Richmond Test of Basic Skills, although an interesting study skill assessment was also used; and the findings are based on observer records of behaviour patterns, rather than the observed individuals' own interpretations of experience.

Nevertheless, the project has provided evidence of a range of primary school teaching styles which is more satisfactory than the use of questionnaire returns and over-generalisations about the formal–informal distinction which had been part of Bennett's (1976) research a few years earlier. Four main types of teaching style were identified in the sample:

22 per cent *individual monitors* (dealing with children individually much of the time, typically using short-lived interactions);

15.5 per cent *class enquirers* (typically highly organised; lucidly making statements of ideas and problems and asking both open and closed questions);

12 per cent *group instructors* (distinguished by giving information to groups to structure their work and then discussing outcomes with them);

50 per cent *style changers* (infrequent changers, habitual changers, rotating changers).

This simple list does not do any kind of justice to the wealth of detail and discussion in the original publication, but several general implications can be drawn for the influences of teaching style on children's performance reported in the second ORACLE volume (Galton and Simon, 1980). One style seems to be especially discredited by the research, the 'rotating changers', where activity areas were set up and children swapped places or materials when the teacher gave a signal. The children being taught by this style came out among the lowest attainers in every test of basic skills and on every study skill except one. The authors of the report judge it as the one style that has little to commend it. Of the other styles, 'class enquirers' were associated with the best performances in mathematics and language but with lower performance on reading than some other groups; the 'group instructors' with good performance in language and acquiring information from tapes and pictures; the 'individual monitors' good performances in reading but among the worst performance in mathematics and language. The 'infrequent changers' did best of all on reading, well on language and maths, but less well on study skills. The 'habitual changers' were associated with the least progress in reading and maths, but best overall on study skills.

The complexity of the findings, even when summarised above, suggests how cautious judgements on the effectiveness of teaching have to be. Some basic findings emerge, notably the importance of smooth routines and the value of open-ended questions. Overall though, the implications of ORACLE are that different styles seem to be more suited to some subject areas and learning activities than others. What may be effective in the teaching of mathematics may not be so effective in generating original writing or in the development of study skills. If there were to be specific recommendations from ORACLE they might well be similar to the one on teaching approach in Southgate's *et al.* (1981) Schools Council report on the dynamic processes affecting reading progress in the extension of beginning reading in twelve schools. From this report, it seems that it is as inappropriate uncritically to adopt an inflexible class teaching approach for all curriculum areas as it is to attempt to individualise all teaching in a class of thirty children. As Gray (1980) remarked in a review of ORACLE, 'the ways of failing as a teacher may be limited but there may be several alternative paths to excellence'. Some of the possible ways of channelling such flexibility of teaching style into helping children develop their writing skills will be set out in succeeding chapters. For the moment, it is worth drawing attention to two specific aspects of classroom conditions for writing, atmosphere and preparatory talk.

CLASSROOM CONDITIONS FOR WRITING

On the basis of his research in junior classrooms, Harpin (1976, p. 138) expresses support for the views of Hourd and Cooper (1959) whose book was discussed in chapter 5. According to these authors the act of writing in a group was particularly beneficial. This heightened attention, engendering slight tension, anticipation and a marked reduction in noise levels. While Harpin acknowledges that pupils obviously vary in their preferences, he concludes that most children seemed to benefit from an awareness of a common activity surrounding them and that 'quiet writing areas' should have as much priority in open plan schools as quiet reading areas.

How much should a topic be talked through before it is written about? Harpin conducted a comparative experiment in which teachers and children talked over topics before beginning writing. In factual writing there seemed to be little effect from the pre-talk, whereas in 'creative writing' the influence of preparatory talk seemed to be to lessen the maturity of the subsequent writing on five out of six measures of linguistic factors such as sentence length, clause length and use of subordinate clauses. Clearly, further research is needed in the whole area of the influence of classroom conditions on writing development, but although specific preparatory talk for children's writing can perhaps boost the confidence of some apprehensive children, it seems best used sparingly. Instead, such attempts to direct talk into what is written can be channelled into the selective interventions proposed in chapter 9.

CHOICE IN WRITING

The final aspect of the classroom context to be dealt with here is the choice allowed to children in what they write. Whereas it may be valuable for them to be regularly involved in writing on topics in which others are similarly engaged, there also seem to be distinctive gains in allowing them some choice. In his doctoral research, carried out in the USA, Graves (1975) found that seven-year-old children given choice wrote more and in greater length than when specific assignments were given. A further finding was that a classroom environment requiring large amounts of 'assigned' writing inhibited the range, content and amount of writing done by children. There has been little equivalent research in the United Kingdom but the later part of this chapter and the one that follows it contain many examples of what children choose to write about if given the opportunity, and the kind of writing which can result.

The following annotated anthology of children's writing has been put together to give an indication of the kinds of task which children can undertake when writing for a variety of aims. Such examples of children's writing are inevitably difficult to appreciate in isolation, so a few details of circumstances are given in most cases, as well as the children's ages, although obviously the nature of the selection should not be taken as indicative of any child's strengths or weaknesses, or of what children of any particular age are capable of.

Examples of children's writing from expressive aims are dealt with in this chapter and the other three main kinds of aims from Kinneavy's framework in the next chapter. At the end of each section of aims some ideas and references are included which may be helpful in extending current work in schools where this is felt to be needed.

THE WRITER: DEVELOPING EXPRESSIVE WRITING

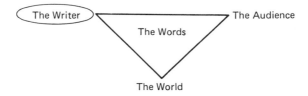

It seems appropriate to begin with the kind of writing which is centrally located in Britton's model and which occupies a vitally important place in Kinneavy's. Kinneavy sees expressive discourse resulting from the use of language as a simple vehicle of expression of some aspect of the 'personality' of the writer. He suggests that expressive elements enter all discourse, but in expressive discourse they are dominant, as in diaries, confessions, or autobiographies. In this type of writing, the distinguishing feature is individuality of style.

Individuality of style can be encouraged in children in their choice of simple titles for what they have written, particularly for autobiographical writing.

Jane forgot her mother's birthday:	'Oh No!'
Colin lost the school hamster:	'Escaped'
The day Hugh fell into the stream:	'Kersplosh'
Elizabeth's house had an extension:	'Utter Chaos'

In many ways, the heart of expressive writing lies in the 'news' tradition of the infant school years. At this stage the sense of personal style may be scarcely discernible, but the articulation of the individual's life experience will be well defined, as with Alison's (6) illustrated account of going into hospital for a tonsil operation.

On Thursday I went in to hospital and played in the play room. Later I went to bed. I tried to get to sleep. The boys were being noisy and I couldn't get to sleep with the noise. The boys got told off by the nurses. one nurse said that she would smack the boys. but the boys didn't stop.

In the later years of primary schooling, expressive writing can be deeply introspective and also symptomatic of a kind of catharsis, in which tensions are released and secrets revealed. Notice the almost parenthetical ending after Mark (8) has come face to face with a fox:

The fox.

I look down the hole. I saw a nose and then some ears. I was looking down a foxes den but i didn't know at the time to me the little fox was like a dog to man. I will always remember up the feild with my freinds up the muddy bank and past the farm. The den was under a big tree with wide spead barnches with big green leaves after ten minuts. I opened my fist what had been closed my hand touched the fox. Then we stw the big fox with brown of red eyes me and my freinds ran down out of the trees back home. This is the onley time i have told any body.

Mark is writing for an audience which is in Britton's terms (see chapter 5, page 55) the teacher (trusted adult), but essentially he seems to be working out the significance for himself. The same seems to be true of Nicola's (9) wistful piece:

A Suprise.

Yesterday I saw a white car drove up behind mummy. Mummy had just been to the town. It was about ten past 6. In the white car was a man, with a face rather like daddys Then I relised that it was daddy. He got out he said hello. I had not daddy for nearly a year. I did not talk to him very much because I were just about to go and play with Elizabeth. I wish I had stayed and talked to him He only stayed for about an hour. because when I came back from Elizabeths he had gone. I wish I could see him more often.

The relationship with the teacher here was extremely 'special' in that she requested that she wanted the contents of the writing 'kept quiet'.

On the other hand, expressive writing can be used in a more celebratory way, such as Kim's (9) rejoicing at reading aloud in the school assembly for the first time.

> My Sish blubbles
>
> On friday morning I was in the Asembly and I was talking about fish and this is wot I sad. last year I got a fish at the fair. I called him blubbles but my mum was was bored of looking aather him So we gave him to Sander and She has Still got him with her other fish She had now they do not no which one is blubbles. on Friday morning When I was in the Asembly I was Shaking and I felt that aather I had read my piece of reading my Skin changed to colour.

There is also a sense of satisfaction and contentment in Jane's (8) diary-like piece:

> AT home I had have put in some plants I have put some wall flowers in a box, I have put in some radishes at the bottom of the garden. the pansies and pearl flowers in the box have not come up yet. Even the tiny shots shoots havent come up but the radishes have got little shoots. there are little red shoots with little bits of green on the end and every day I oth watch the radishes.

The circumstances of all these pieces of writing were total freedom of choice of subject matter, as part of the compilation of folders of personal writing on which the children worked most days of the week. The general issue of assessment and marking will be left until chapter 9, but expressive writing in the above conditions may be most appropriately treated in the context which spawned it. As the context is personally centred on the writer, the response of the teacher may well be best focused on the writer as a person and channelled into a similarly personal, expressive reply, written or spoken. A personal folder allows children the opportunity to explore the possibilities and intrinsic rewards of writing without the danger of being constrained by fear of correction of flaws identified by the application of objective criteria. Such criteria are in many ways inappropriate in the subjective world of much expressive writing which may represent children's attempts to capture a 'stream of consciousness', in words, for their own satisfaction.

It has to be admitted that children may initially find it difficult to adjust to the personal choices which opportunities for expressive writing allow. This rather paradoxical situation can be met by prompting them to consider such topics as likes and dislikes, favourite things or worst experiences. The writing from such prompts may be given a greater precision if children are encouraged to identify the audience for whom they are writing.

The next two pieces of writing resulted from children recalling a memorable experience and shaping it in an entertaining way for the others in the class. Susan (10) remembers the day a neighbour's little girl walked:

Baby Karen

When I first saw Karen she was so tiny. She had no to hair. She cried when she was hungry hungry. Karen had no teeth. Just a baby. But she was taught to crawl Crawling everywhere. Bashing into chairs. Crying because her gums hurt when she was teething. Her mother bought Karen a Baby Walker. Crashing into the furniture. But one day Thursday, I put Karen down on the floor. To my amaze-ment Karen walked straight across the floor! My sister screamed and Karen fell down with fright. She did it again and again. She was walking!

James (10) recalls the day he bled the radiators at home:

> My father had told me to let the air out of the radiators when I got home. I fetched the key and started to let the air out, but when I got to the fourth bedroom radiator the end came off. I put my foot over it and then called for help, my mum rushed up and put her thumb over the hole. Water was gushing out and mum sent me to bed. She couldn't stop me because she had to keep her thumb over the hole. She was shouting all sorts of things at me. That was a day I shall never forget!

Where children know that they are going to be involved in unusual experiences, they can be 'contracted' to maintain the kind of diary or put together the kind of report which will appeal to others in the class. This was the case with the diary that Sunil kept on his visit to India, which also included photographs and drawings when it was made available for his classmates back in England. (He was 11.)

Tuesday

... and back to school with my two cousins. Neilum and me, no friends to play with, so we spent our day playing, and me working until we went to market. To catch a bus in India you have to run like Steve Ovett, and then it stops in the middle of the road, plus the bus is always full, so you have to grab anything you can get hold of. When we got off our taxi instead of a bus we liked what we saw and took hours looking for the right material. At last we got back to our house and after thirty minutes went back out again to see the beating of the retreat for Republic Day. About five thousand people were watching the bands perform. About four hundred were performing and it was quite good, then all of us went home and the motor bikes were ruling the roads again.

Extending opportunities for expressive writing

This kind of approach may be well established where teachers have recognised the value of the opportunities for expressive writing argued in the Bullock Report. Kinneavy, though, goes a little further than Bullock in making a distinction between 'individual' and 'social' expressive writing. The latter can be a promising way of extending children's involvement in expressive writing and incorporating recently-published ideas on the use of journalistic types of activities in schools.

Again the sense of audience can be both a key incentive and a crucial influence upon the register adopted. See, for example, the way in which this group of ten- to 11-year-olds have tried to appeal to the other campers in this school camp newsheet and to make the best of arriving in the rain by the use of neologisms ('invermation') and hyperbole ('his shocking behaviour').

```
The editors of TOP TIMES newspaper hope you are having a nice time
even though the weather was not so nice on Monday.  We are very
sorry about the weather and that you had to go home on Tuesday.  Now
that you are back we hope the weather is nice until Friday.  The
TOP TIMES newspaper will give you all the invermation you will need.
.............................
```

```
This picture is just a little 'Thank you', and a sign of a new-made
friendship.
           .............................
```

```
Whilst getting change for the 'phone, I met the Squire and explained
why we missed the Hegg Nurdling.  He realised his dreadful mistake,
said how brave we were to survive the night, and regretted his
shocking behaviour.  He hopes to make it up to us later in the week.
```

In an entertaining and practical little book, Andrews and Noble (1982) show how the skills of elementary journalism may be incorporated into children's writing, especially where it is group based. Although designed for secondary schools, its ideas could be easily adapted to work with top junior and middle school children. The main concern of the book is with editing and it deals with such possibilities as classroom magazines, novels

Assembly Incident.

1 Ring bell (fire alarm) people think it
is time to go down, In fact
real fire.

2 OHP blows up. PANIC. screen
falls down on people MORE PANIC.

3 Assem, April fools day. gang
put out wrong. hymn ~~books~~,
loosen screws on screen so
falls down. Put wrong fuse
in OHP blows up, Old chairs
leg broken for fat teachers.
grease on floor? Mile.

4 Bomp in Roof.

teachers stand, release mice, only
chairs in sight broken ones. ~~for~~
fat teachers. Gym display,
special mat with tacks in. A

Interview With head.
Vandelism, vandals ~~caught~~, Interv,
they take no notice, Head
takes revenge.

Ghost. Tells head what to
do

and plays as well as suggestions on the kind of notation techniques which can be used in proof reading.

See how Craig (12) has planned his entertaining spoof for a school newsheet in note form and used another member of the class as trial audience for the first full draft.

First draft.

The Assembly Incident

It was April 1st and the bell for assembly had just gone, and already people were lining up, "Well" said Mrs Fattersnob, our extremely fat teacher, "I don't know whats got into you, you seem in a real hurry to get down to assembly. Is something going on?" Little did she know.

We proceeded on, down to the hall and formed up into orderly lines. I shuffled closer to the rest of the gang. "all set", "yes", "this should be fun" BE QUIET! 4 F roared Mr Bigborg the head. We hung our heads in mock shame and tried not to laugh.

"As you know today is April fools day and Im very pleased to hear that their has been no monkey business, as a treat for this assembly will only be 40 minutes long". Waffled Bigbor, "now let us sing" at which point the O.H.P. was switched on and Bigbor rifled off the first few lines of morning has broken only to be cut short by the hoots of laughter, from the children, "What, what is the meaning of this" he turned and looked at the screen, there on the screen was a large picture of a nude baby labeled "baby Bigbor".

[Marginal annotations: "Funny Name" (pointing to Fattersnob); "am'e? perhaps good but" (pointing to "mock")]

8 Other aims in writing: the words, the world and the audience

This chapter continues the exploration of possibilities of developing children's writing by adopting different aims, again by applying Kinneavy's framework. Three further aims are considered: 'literary', where the emphasis is on the written product; 'referential', where the emphasis is on the world which is being written about; and 'persuasive', where the emphasis is on getting the audience or receiver of the writing to do or believe something. The examples of children's writing and the brief commentaries should be helpful in planning work in schools and each section ends with some suggestions for extending this work in a number of directions.

THE WORDS ON THE PAGE: DEVELOPING 'LITERARY' WRITING

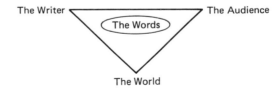

Writing which has literary aims is writing where the structure of the writing is made a priority and is worthy of being appreciated in its own right (Kinneavy, 1971, p. 39). For this to occur, Kinneavy argues, the structure of the language is likely to be made conspicuous and it is likely to have 'unity' and 'fit'.

The whole range of the linguistic features outlined in chapter 3 can be made conspicuous, as in rhyme, alliteration ('two tremendous tigers'), figures of speech, or the organisation of the text. Writing with other aims obviously uses conspicuous structures at times, but they are the *raison d'être* of literary writing.

'Unity' can exist horizontally through rhythm, symbolism and setting;

and also vertically in the flow through the texts. Unity can be important in the fulfilment of other written aims, but literary unity is generally of a more rigid kind. Scientific reports can be abstracted, newspaper articles edited, but if novels, poetry or songs are abbreviated or summarised, their artistic heart is mutilated or destroyed, such is the organic unity of their structures.

According to Kinneavy, the conspicuous and unified structures of literary writing must also have 'fitness' or 'harmony' in which the form of the language is congruent with some kind of current convention. Some of these characteristics can be seen in the extracts which follow but, as Kinneavy suggests, they can be an integral part of a whole variety of stories, poetry, songs, plays and jokes.

Graham's (9) writing on going into his school during the summer holidays exemplifies some of these characteristics. There is an overriding emphasis on the two four-line structures, there is unity of setting, rhythm (more or less), exclamatory fourth lines and the piece is generally harmonious with the conventions of blank verse.

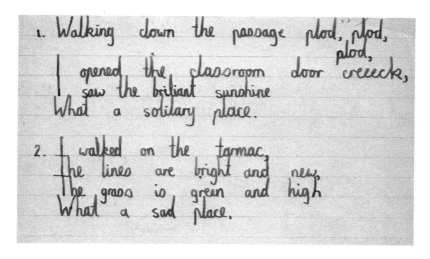

1. Walking down the passage plod, plod, plod,
   I opened the classroom door creeeck,
   I saw the briliant sunshine
   What a solitary place.

2. I walked on the tarmac,
   The lines are bright and new,
   The grass is green and high
   What a sad place.

Literary writing includes the kind generally called 'creative' in the publications reviewed in chapter 5, in which children are encouraged to include vocabulary and imagery in unusually 'vivid' ways. The dangers of indulgent over-writing from such an approach can be seen in Martin's (9) and Bridget's (10) pieces on Autumn and there are indications from their inclusion of what the teacher had made clear was a 'good word' ('tranquility') that these pieces come from the same lesson.

The stimulus-response model of a narrowly conceived 'creative writing' lesson seems best used sparingly. Perhaps it can be most profitably linked to a sympathetic commentary by the teacher on the possibilities of structure, unity and harmony in writing, rather than a concentration on teacher-approved words and phrases. Linking writing to an evolving

The Autumn tranquility is not broken by the gay twitter of the summer birds. Now only a few stray birds fly the sky us the lone cowboys riding in the desolate desert. Little animals scurry to their burrows for they fear they will become frozen in the winter snows. A thin layer of fog is hanging about the swaying trees. Jack frost chokes the flowers until they die.

curriculum theme can provide indirect resources and experiences on which young writers can draw. At the same time, to reject the creative writing lesson entirely seems unnecessarily extreme. In the same lesson as the one reported above, Clare (9) (opposite, below) has been less influenced by teacher preparation and has produced a memorable last line.

Tranquility dominated the Autumn evening except for the crackle of a few leaves falling every now and then from the towering trees.

The pond glistened in the silence and most of the weary pond creatures were asleep with only a few hidden in the weeds. At that moment the moons blurred reflection was on the pond. It looked like millions of diamonds that had been smuggled out out of another country to England on a silent night when the soft quick ripples of the salty sea water were lapping

The sky is dull and grey, the trees look sad as they stand in the cold Autumn wind. Dead leaves cover the ground with a brown carpet. Children in warm wooley clothes collect shiny brown conkers. Bang! go fireworks lighting up the stale sky. Then after all the bonfires have burnt to cinders, all goes old and dull again. The muddy grass is no longer a fresh green. The Autumn has come and haunted everything with sadness.

A less narrow approach is to raise children's awareness of the possibilities of language of a literary type which they can try out over a period of time. The following three came from a local study based on a home-made nature trail, designed to introduce some significant areas of study in physical geography and natural history. Deborah (10) set herself the task of writing within a visual structure to represent a tree in the school grounds. Carl (9) opted for rhyming poetry when writing about clouds.

Lombardy Poplar

A massive great hulk
of a tree. Looking too
proud to talk to any
tree smaller than himself.
Dark and thick with
an inner mind and
feeling. The dark foliage
enclosing the trunk. Its
leaves looking out of
place when one is on
his own. It looks
mysterious and sturdy. It
makes me feel like an
insect and it has
always impressed me.
It looks as if
it will never stop
advancing into the
sky an then fall
and crush the
world

Clouds

Firey nimbus raging up high
And fluffy warm cumulus slowly passing by.

And many more pleasures the clouds bring across
What would happen if we found their loss?

There is cirrus like cobwebs of snow,
There are the other ones where do they go?

All the clouds in the sky like mountains of wool
Like baskets of flour when they're very full.

The study of the stream running through school grounds prompted Hugh (10) to write a story for the rest of the class. This kind of consciously planned 'writing for others' can lead to some very original illustrations, as this example shows.

The six-page story began:

Dwarfs Wooden Raft Adventure

It was the fist day of July and dwarf was listening to his favorite radio programme called 'Desert Island Dicks, he lived in suringwell and had a tree stump as a home. Then he had a super idea, or an idea that he thought was super, but you might not think it super when you hear about it but he did so I'll leave it at that. Then he got up and switched off the radio because he wanted to start on his idea right away and not waste time. Now, his super idea was to build a raft and have an adventure on the stream that was flowing past his home. He went out and started to collect some sticks that were straight and strong (sticks to him were as big as logs to people). After that he went out to find some-thing to keep the sticks together, after he had been out for some time he came across a tube of plastic glue and the five minutes later two liquorice sticks. He took them back to his tree stump. He started building right away and nearly used up all the glue sticking his sticks together, then to make sure it was really stronghe wound the liquorice sticks around it. "Now I'm almost ready he said to himself", "I only need a paddle now and a little cabin". So he collected more sticks and started to make a little cabin a the back, when it was finished the walls sloped into point at the top. Then he fixed on a flag. He carved a paddle with a penknife he had found two weeks ago

It ended:

He used the chewing gum as glue and stuck the cardboard on leaving a little gap at the top so that he could put the mattres in and get in himself. Then he rolled it back in with his bed in it and it floated well. He got in and started paddling, it would be harder to move forward now because he was going against the current. When he got about half way home, water started leaking through the chewing gum and he had to get up and find something to patch it up, he found a big glob of honey but he got it garmed all over the roof of his raft and he had to find something else to use and he found some bit of cork so he took them back and stuck the bits to the chewing gum where the leaks were. When he got home he was glad to see his old friends again. He made up his mind neve to go on a raft again because he'd wasted a tube of plastic glue and two liquorice sticks and had to come home in a boat that was half a detergent bottle garmed with honey and chewing gum lost a hat and nearly been eaten by a lizard. He told all his friends about the adventure downstream and some of them were jelous and tried to do something exiting to.

Extending opportunities for literary writing

Two recent sources of ideas have provided some very promising possibilities for fostering the growth of literary writing in schools. One is a direct source of practical ideas on the teaching of poetry from Sandy Brownjohn (1980) which introduces general ideas for teaching (e.g. introductory poetry games) and more direct advice on specific techniques, some of them of an advanced kind (e.g. riddles, acrostics, haiku and sonnets). Some of the advice glosses over complex issues (for example, 'correct grammar'), but it does contain a number of straightforward practical ideas, as does an even more recent book by the same author (Brownjohn, 1982).

The second development is the overdue recognition in some quarters of the potential which children's literature has for generating many avenues of work throughout the curriculum. The need for teachers and parents to recognise the deep-seated psychological gains of engaging in literature has been recently endorsed by the DES (1982b). This suggestion is very pertinent here, for literature is one of the principal avenues of literary writing. Moreover, as is noted elsewhere in this book, the past quarter century or so has been seen as a 'golden age' of children's literature. How far regular reading and hearing of stories and poetry can indirectly influence children's writing has not yet been effectively researched. The Bradford Book Flood Project (Ingham, 1982), which assessed the effect of making large numbers of additional books available to middle school children, has highlighted the complex relationships of the factors involved. These include the knowledge and attitudes of parents and teachers, how the books are made available and the reactions of family and friends.

A school-based book flood could be a very worthwhile strategy for a school to adopt as a permanent feature of its work. Multiple copies of cheaper paperback editions could be introduced into classrooms, read in part or whole to groups or classes of children and made available for children to turn to in their own voluntary silent reading. Such an approach could act as a catalyst in school-focused in-service activities which might lead to discussions on such matters as techniques of book promotion, ways of involving families, the place of silent reading in the school day and the ways of assessing influences on reading and writing. Centrally important would be the choice of books to be used in the flood and those chosen could be changed or reviewed from time to time.

My own starter list for a school-based book flood is given below. I have limited the number of books to six per two-year age-range and have not included more than one book per author, even though some warrant several different inclusions. I have also limited the choice to books which are available in paperback, some with more than one publisher, except for some of the poetry anthologies, of which there is one in each age-range. An excellent but relatively cheap publication to help teachers and parents become more knowledgeable on what is available for children is *The Good Book Guide to Children's Books* (Taylor and Braithwaite, 1983).

Pre-school

This Little Puffin compiled by Elizabeth Matterson (Kestrel, also Puffin – both Penguin Books)

Each Peach, Pear, Plum by Janet and Allan Ahlberg (Armada Picture Lions – Collins)

Mr Gumpy's Outing by John Burningham (Puffin – Penguin Books)

Sunshine by Jan Ormerod (Puffin – Penguin Books)

Mr Brown Can Moo, Can You? by Dr Seuss (Beginner Books – Collins)

But Where is the Green Parrot? by Thomas and Wanda Zacharias (Piccolo – Pan Books)

5–7

The Mother Goose Treasury illustrated by Raymond Briggs (Hamish Hamilton; also Puffin – Penguin Books)

Mr Magnolia by Quentin Blake (Armada Picture Lions – Collins)

The Very Hungry Caterpillar by Eric Carle (Puffin – Penguin Books)

The Wind Blew by Pat Hutchins (Puffin – Penguin Books)

The Tiger who Came to Tea by Judith Kerr (Armada Picture Lions – Collins)

Where the Wild Things Are by Maurice Sendak (Puffin – Penguin Books)

7–9

I Like This Poem edited by Kaye Webb (Kestrel, also Puffin – both Penguin Books)

The Enormous Crocodile by Roald Dahl (Puffin – Penguin Books)

The Shrinking of Treehorn by Florence Parry Heide (Puffin – Penguin Books)

Dogger by Shirley Hughes (Armada Picture Lions – Collins)

The Iron Man by Ted Hughes (Faber Paperbacks)

The Owl who was Afraid of the Dark by Jill Tomlinson (Puffin – Penguin Books)

9–11

Wordscapes compiled by Barry Maybury (Oxford University Press)

The Turbulent Term of Tyke Tiler by Gene Kemp (Puffin – Penguin Books)

The Lion, the Witch and the Wardrobe by C. S. Lewis (Armada Lions – Collins)

The Ghost of Thomas Kempe by Penelope Lively (Piccolo – Pan Books)

The Battle of Bubble and Squeak by Philippa Pearce (Puffin – Penguin Books)

Charlotte's Web by E. B. White (Puffin – Penguin Books)

11–13

Dragonsteeth edited by Eric Williams (Edward Arnold)

John Diamond by Leon Garfield (Puffin – Penguin Books)

Elidor by Alan Garner (Armada – Collins)

Charmed Life by Diane Wynne Jones (Puffin – Penguin Books)
Mrs Frisby and the Rats of NIMH by Robert C. O'Brien (Puffin – Penguin Books)
The Hobbit by J. R. R. Tolkien (Unwin Paperbacks)

THE WORLD: DEVELOPING 'REFERENTIAL' WRITING

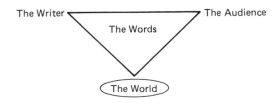

Referential writing, in Kinneavy's analysis, is that which 'designates or reproduces reality'. He accepts that the term 'expository' is more commonly used for such writing, but argues that exposition is more a matter of what is said than why it is said. Therefore he puts forward 'referential' as more appropriate for use in his network of aims and expository is identified as a mode, although it does not appear in Kinneavy's set of four modes (see chapter 5). Nevertheless, if the term 'expository' is felt to be more appropriate, the following section could be reasonably read as an exploration of possibilities for expository writing with children, providing that this is coupled with an acceptance of exposition as an aim.

Kinneavy also sub-divides into three the aim of writing which predominantly makes reference to the world: 'exploratory' writing involves seeking the nature of the reality of the world; 'informative' writing simply relays a reality which is conceived as 'known'; 'scientific' writing goes beyond this and systematically adds 'proof' of the validity of this information.

Opportunities for the use of exploratory writing will occur when children are involved in such activities as surveys, interviews, or genuinely open discussions. Older children in primary schools are capable of planning and administering adventurous surveys which may in turn engender an appropriate sense of caution towards both the creation of evidence and the kinds of generalisations which can be made from it. This may have occurred in the fourth year junior class whose survey report appeared in a school magazine in the following form:

<u>The Birth of our Survey</u>

Our survey started with our class discussing subjects which cause many arguments in Parliament and among the general public. We were interested by the different opinions over the subjects at home, so we decided to find out exactly what the general public really thought.

The Questions:-

We had to sort out eight subjects out of a list of fifteen
to write questions for. The final eight were -

Streaming.   Competition in school work.
Competition in school sport.   Comprehensive schools.
Arming the Police.   The death penalty.
Sex education.   Space exploration.

We were careful not to choose subjects that might embarrass or
offend anyone such as religion or apartheid. We compiled the
questions and copied them into our note-books.

The questions were -

1. Do you think children should be put into classes according to
   their ability?

2. Do you think competition in school work is good or bad?

3. Are you for or against competition in school sport?

4. Are you for or against comprehensive schools?

5. Do you think our police force should be armed?

6. Do you think the death penalty should be re-introduced?

7. Do you think sex-education should be taught in Junior Schools?

8. Do you think too much money is being spent on space exploration?

Each of us had to ask at least ten people these questions. We
were also told to get answers from a cross-section of the public e.g.
pensioners, doctors, ordinary workers and housewives.

CONCLUSION

We found that not many people wanted any change in life except
a change in the death penalty and sex education. We were rather
surprised at the number against sex education. The public were
divided on their opinions over Comprehensive schooling, and we also
found that old age pensioners did not want any change in life and
they all seemed to think alike. The remainder of the adults had
widely differing opinions and gave unpredictable answers.

A third year junior class surveyed the traffic passing the main entrance to
the school during 8.30 am and 4.30 pm. Pairs of children took thirty-
minute turns on the survey and then different groups compiled and
presented the results.

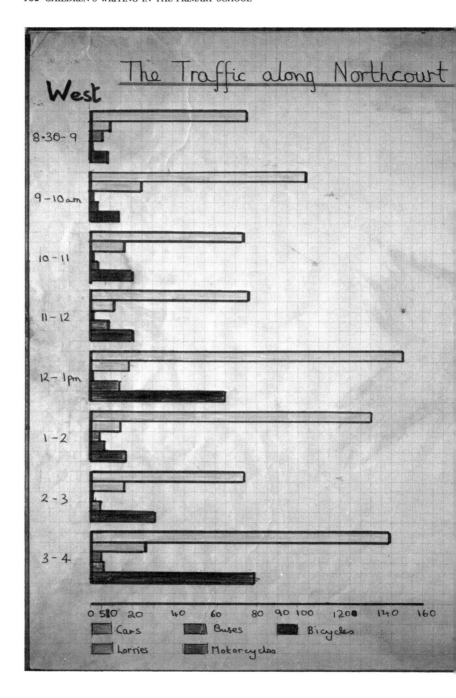

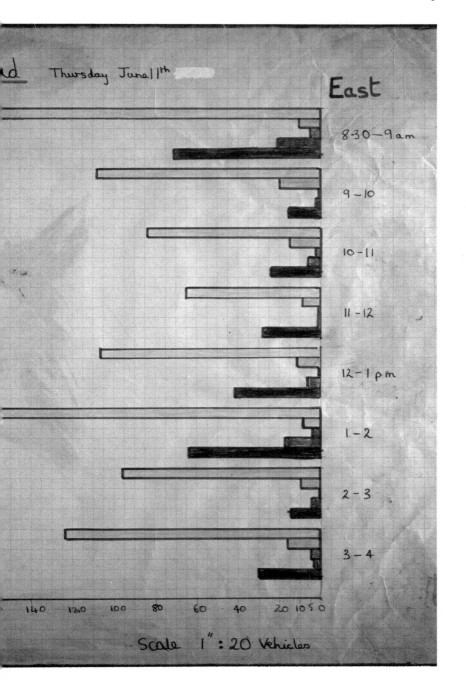

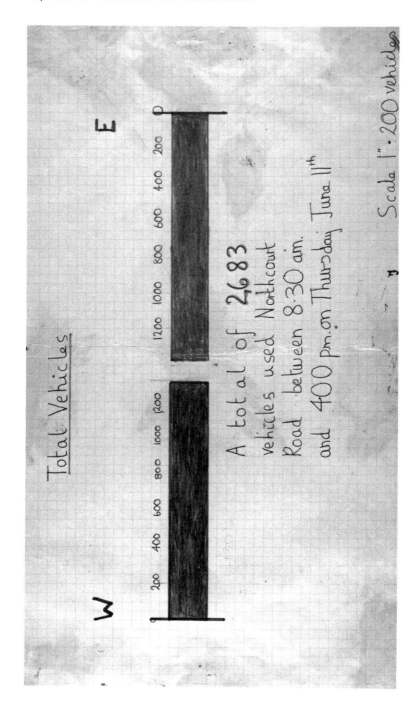

Total Vehicles

A total of 2683 vehicles used Northcourt Road between 8.30 am. and 4.00 pm. on Thursday June 11th

Scale 1" . 200 vehicles

'Informative' writing can spring from visits to places of general interest to other children, such as Gillian's (10) report of a school visit to Wiltshire.

West Kennet Long Barrow

A long barrow is a very ancient burial place, in fact it was used near the end of Neolithic times and into the Bronze Age. It was a tribal or family tomb. When they buried the people they gave them a little gift to carry them on their journey into the next world. When the tribe thought they had buried enough bodies they sealed the tomb up with sarsen stones or smaller ones.

On Friday when we went on our visit, we visited the West Kennet Long Barrow. The length of it was about 350 feet. We were allowed to go into it. Inside it was very dark and smelly. The boys in our class were scaring the girls and we were screaming.

A 'model' of the solar system made by a class of eight- and nine-year-olds attracted attention from classes through the school. Graham, Clare and Kim (all 8) put together this information for the children and teachers who came to view it.

How we made our Solar System

In Class 2S we have made a model of the Solar System on our ceiling. To do this we had to collect nine plastic balls and we put one layer of papier mache with water on them, and then we put layers of newspaper alternately with glue. When the balls were dry we cut open the papier mache and took out each ball. Then we stuck the two halves back together again. We painted them their right colours. To make the sun, we put lots of screwed-up newspaper on a circle of polystyrene and stuck paper towels over the top. We painted our sun yellow. We hung them all up by cotton and cup hooks. We did this by borrowing Mr. Marriott's decorating apparatus. But before we did this, we drew the orbits with a rubber on a string. Everybody had a turn on the apparatus. We made the asteroids from drawing-pins. The model looks very nice on the ceiling. If it was not for Mr. Beard, who organised the whole thing, there would never have been Heaven in our classroom!

'Scientific' writing may be a rather exaggerated term for the attempts of children to describe reality systematically and support their descriptions with reference to valid evidence. However, there can be distinctive beginnings in the descriptions based on the careful observations of things which hold their attention. Dawn (7) made a detailed examination of a daffodil:

My daffodil
Daffodils are
yellow and green.
They have a stem
and a Flower.
The shape of
the Flower
is like a stemx
star with a
bell on the Front.
The petals Feel
like silk. At the
end of the bell
it is all crinkley

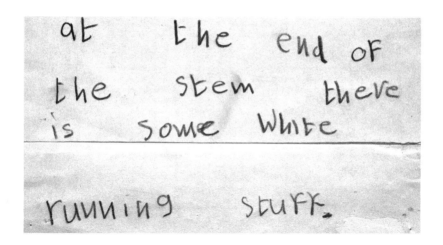

at the end of
the stem there
is some White

running stuff.

Jonathan (11) took a very close look at some cow parsley and his report is extremely detailed and continually related to what his inspections revealed:

I have been out to get some cow parsley. I picked two plants - one with and one without roots. I have decided to start examining the roots. The main root looks to me like an old dried whitish carrot. Small roots of the same kind grow off the side. The end of the root comes to a point. The surface of the root looks very much like the bark of a tree. I have cut the root in two parts. Inside it is a cream colour with a white centre. The centre acts as a core because you can peel the cream part off, so just the white centre is left. The skin of the root is very tough. Now that I have cut the root, the room smells as if someone has been making something with spice. Above the roots, the stem is very hard and I can not cut it. I have just cut it about one inch further up. There is no longer a white centre. It is hollow with a white pith. The outside now has small white hairs all over it. I have just come across some small black insects in the hollow part of the stem. I have just chewed the stem. It tastes like ginger. I have come to the first stem branching off the main one. There also seems to be a double layer of thin skin where the smaller stem joins the main one. Each leaf comes to a point at the top. The front of the leaf is a lot darker than the back. I looked at a flower under a magnifying glass. The centre of the flower is a lovely lime colour. I took five flowers and counted the petals. These are my results: five, five, five, six, six. On one small slender stem approximately fifteen flowers grow. The buds which have no signs of flowers look like Aniseed. The other plant was a lot younger. It was not hollow but it had a hard green jelly in it.

There are also embryonic features of 'scientific' writing in Martin's predictions from a project which involved seeking the help of a local RAF station. Fifty weather balloons bearing return labels were inflated and released in front of all the children in the school on a day when an extremely strong north-easterly wind was blowing. Martin (10) wondered whether any balloons would reach Brussels where a party of children were soon to go on an educational visit.

UP, UP AND AWAY

```
On Monday, we let our balloons go.
Flight Sergeants Ellerbeck and Wardle from R.A.F. Abingdon filled the
balloons with hydrogen, a light gas.
The balloons rose at a rate of 200 feet per minute, travelling at an
average speed of 90 m.p.h.  The balloons will burst at a height of
35,000 ft.  My calculations tell me that it will take approx 2hrs 40
mins., to get from here to Brussels (it's 240 miles away).
Forty balloons were let up.
Here are my calculations.          20
                2       r6=2 6/9 = 2⅔ ∅∅ x ²/₁ = 40m
            9∅ /24∅
                18
                ─
                6

SO it will take 2hrs 40 mins, going at 90 m.p.h.  We hope that one
will land in Belgium.  One was found in Sellwood Road just outside
the school.  Simon made a witty remark and said "It should have
landed in Holland Road."  Corny isn't it?
```

(In fact one label was returned from a farmhouse in the Netherlands and a party of children did make a detour to visit it as part of their stay on the continent. A little later another label was returned from Poland.)

There are similar embryonic indications in Alison's (10) calculations and account after a matchstick was thrown into the stream which ran through the school grounds. The stream was a tributary of the Thames and the beginning of its 'journey to London' was timed to help 'estimate' the time when it would pass the Houses of Parliament. Alison also painted a picture of the 'end' of this unusual journey to London.

Extending opportunities for referential writing

Of the possibilities for extending current work in the broad area of referential writing, two seem especially promising. Both are from recent work in two universities which are very involved in research and development in educational institutions.

At the Centre for the Study of Human Learning at Brunel University, studies have been undertaken over several years into 'learning referents'. Such studies have generally given priority to gaining access to the meanings that individuals attach to experiences in ways which also allow for structured comparisons of differences within and between people over time.

The match travelled 6yds in 12 seconds

" " 1yd in $\frac{12}{6} = 2$ seconds

" " 1760 yds in 2×1760 secs.
(1 mile) $= 3520$ seconds.

" " 1 mile in $60\overline{)3250}$

" " 60 miles in $60\overline{)3520} \frac{\times 60 =}{3520 \text{ mins}}$

" " 60 miles in $60\overline{)3520}$
58hr 4
minutes

The match left our field at 12 noon on Tuesday 20th May.
It will reach London, 60 miles away at twenty minutes to eleven on Tuesday night.

These are part of a series of investigations into 'learning conversations' in which individuals are helped to make sense of learning experiences in ways which may improve future learning strategies (Thomas and Harri-Augstein, 1976).

Learning 'referents' play a central role in the awareness-raising, reflection and self-monitoring involved, when individuals try to encapsulate, normally in writing, the essence of what they have learned; this writing acts as a negotiated focus in the 'learning conversation' between learner and teacher or counsellor. In the research undertaken at the Centre with adults, referents have included flow diagrams, personal taxonomies and records of reading behaviour (Harri-Augstein *et al.*, 1982). Properly to exploit the potential of this kind of individualised learning perspective for primary and middle school children, it can be effectively coupled with the explorations by Merritt (1977) and his colleagues at the Open University of various kinds of diagrammatic outcomes from reading, such as lists, tables, charts, plans, tree diagrams and various types of matrix and graph. Recent research in the same university has indicated that the use of such referents can increase children's reading comprehension (Sheldon, 1982).

THE AUDIENCE: DEVELOPING PERSUASIVE WRITING

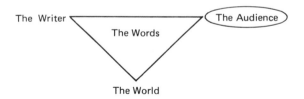

Persuasive writing will be used when the emphasis is on the person for whom the writing is intended. In Kinneavy's (1971, p. 39) words, 'encoder, reality and language itself all become instrumental to the achievement of some practical effect in the decoder'. In the context of writing, persuasive writing can arise when the intended audience has a different attitude from that of the writer. Consequently, persuasive writing can include attempts to make an alternative view plausible by the use of apparent logic and proof. There may be emotional terms and references.

An obvious example of persuasive writing which pervades our lives is advertising. The sophisticated linguistic strategies used by advertisers deserve more attention than they often receive in schools. Some of the many possibilities for bringing their study into the curriculum are set out by Williams (1976) and Hoffman (1976).

The awareness of the use of puns in advertisements is likely to be increased by children devising their own, such as these put together by a fourth year junior class (manufacturers' names omitted):

If you want to get the point buy a .... pencil.
Get her in a sweet mood. Give her a ....
You never make a mistake when you buy a .... rubber.
Get on the right track with .... running shoes.
Don't lose your grip. Use .... tyres.
Don't lose your head. Wear a .... crash helmet.
Get a cut above the others with .... scissors.

Persuasive writing can develop from children's involvement with displays and exhibitions. The following piece of work came spontaneously from Sandra (10) to put on the classroom door for the school open day. During the afternoon parents were invited to wander through the school, calling in at classrooms which caught their eye and where the children were still at work.

For you

1 Come on in. your welcome today,
Look on the wall and see the
pictures gay.

2 And also some writing all of
different thing's,
Pictures of birds and their
feathery wing's.

3 When you have finished, there's our
Story Book,
Do come on in and have a look!

4 There are curvy patterns and
Straight one's too,
We have put them all up especially
for you.

Possibilities in persuasive writing may only become fully apparent to children if they are immersed in realistic tasks to try to argue a case at some length. Notice Paul's (13) impassioned argument, use of precise examples and range of syntactical devices in trying to make his middle school classmates more aware of current manifestations of cruelty to animals.

How on earth can so-called humans murder seals who used to swim happily and stare lovingly at their mothers, in the arctic wastes and in Canada. That was only until they came with their clubs and gave the seals terrible deaths. After all, ladies don't have to have their fur coats, made from a living animals skin. Some countries have banned the cull, but isn't it about time that the rest of the world came to their senses.

Staying in a cold climate, the next issue is whaling. There have been several "Save the Whale" protests, which very rightly disapprove of the harpooning of these giant, graceful creatures. What minds must these murderous men have, who kill an already disappearing animal.

In 1982, Japanese hunters deliberately slaughtered a herd of dolphins that got washed up onto the beaches. Everyone thought that they would carry out the normal procedure: stripping of skin, but they didn't. Even after questioning, the men didn't give a reason why, so this is a cold blooded murder. People like this must be stopped.

Fox hunting is one of the most popular, but also most cruel bloodsports. Just put yourself in the place of the fox, and imagine how terrified you would be, with horses, men and hounds after you. When the fox has been caught, bitten and killed, its head, tail and feet are cut off. Now do you agree with this torture.

Experiments are one of the most horrifying
things of all. Countless murders of innocent animals
take place each day. Animals who had lives to lead.
Here are some examples of the experiments.
* Calves have electronic sensors placed inside them.
  The hole from the operation is not stitched up.
* Dogs are pumped full of alcohol until they burst.
* Rabbits have perfume dropped into their eyes.
  That could be your dog or rabbit. Now join the
organizations in their fight to ban experiments.
  Another point is that people are very often biased. A
nice, fluffy puppy will be stroked and petted, but an
ugly spider will be trodden into the ground. These, and
all the other animals, I have mentioned have a right
to enjoy life while they can, so why don't we let them.

Extending opportunities for persuasive writing

Of the four aims for writing being discussed here, that of persuasion is
likely to be especially dependent upon the appropriateness of the context
which the teacher engineers. In some ways, this is the most demanding
writing aim for young children and there are indications that they find it
easier to undertake from about nine onwards (Wilkinson et al., 1980;
Bereiter and Scardamalia, 1982). Persuasive writing carries with it the
need to decentre sufficiently to take up the viewpoint of someone else and
continually to relate the writing to it. It also demands that the writer adopts
structures, such as the use of reasons, appeals and concessions, which may
not have been heard or read so often compared with others commonly
found in writing resulting from other aims.

Again, this is an aspect of writing development which is very much in
need of reliable research. One or two modest suggestions seem worth
making. It seems likely that children will engage themselves in persuasive
writing most readily if the task is genuine and credible. This condition may
be met within the basic context of the school, where there is some mild
controversy or local issue, perhaps. It may also help if the viewpoint of the
audience is made explicitly clear, in the form of writing which is freely
available or a version of it abstracted into a list or summary. The need for
young writers to spell out their persuasive arguments may be sharpened by
a formal presentation of some kind, in which the writing can be read to the

audience in question and an oral debate built around the different contributions. It is within such contexts of realistic and clearly specified writing tasks that the teacher can best make the planned teaching interventions to foster the development of the various components of writing which are explored in the next chapter.

9 Assessing and improving writing

Although so much writing goes on in schools and a range of books have been published on it, the assessment of writing has received relatively little attention and a good deal less than the assessment of reading (e.g. Pumfrey, 1976; Vincent and Cresswell, 1976) or even the appraisal of the use of spoken language (e.g. Tough, 1976).

Understandably, the core of assessment tends to be centred largely on marking and correcting, but it is important to return to the overall view of the writing process (outlined in chapter 3) to deal adequately with the task of assessing it. Only when this kind of broad perspective is adopted can the issues of assessing and teaching writing be approached in a properly 'professional' way.

Fundamental to this perspective is the distinction between composing and transcribing, the 'what' and the 'how' of writing. The 'why' of writing must always be borne in mind too, as a consideration of identifying the aim in using this time-consuming and rather contrived language skill is central to creating a sensitive context for assessment. If instead a response to the meanings composed in writing, or to the intention of the writer is subjugated to a meticulous but exclusive concentration on the details of the product, such as its punctuation, then the pupil can be caught up in a narrowly conceived series of 'inspections'.

The dangers of over-detailed concentration on marking, as opposed to constructive assessment, are seen in a book on secondary school practices by Dunsbee and Ford (1980). In a very interesting part of the book, the school writing of one boy from all five of his secondary school years is used as a case study for discussion. The general conclusion to be drawn from this sample is that the boy's writing was consistently inspected for flaws, was rarely praised and is likely to have left the boy feeling that writing is 'a chore and dangerous in the way it makes him vulnerable to attack' (Dunsbee and Ford, 1980, p. 40).

How far such an example is typical of trends in the primary school is not easy to say, but the dangers of any teacher adopting an over-zealous, fault-finding approach to marking children's writing must be carefully weighed up. Moreover, considerations on the marking of children's writing seem better set against the broader context of what is known about the nature of the writing process, whatever the age-range of the children. Broader considerations of this kind need to take full account of what lies behind the words on the page, such as how it seems to have been composed. The ordering of the words into syntactical patterns which are appropriate to the task may need to be considered, as well as other features of the general area of 'register' that was described in chapter 3. All this can be part of a more broadly-based assessment of the growth of children's writing ability both through the increase in the use of different language features and as different aims are attempted. More fundamentally still, there is much to be said in favour of closely involving children themselves in this whole process of assessment, seeking their views and encouraging them in self-criticism.

Providing that this overall perspective is continually borne in mind, it can be useful to examine how each of these aspects can be effectively assessed over time, how children's weaknesses and potentials can be recognised and helped, and to consider the implications for a teacher's approach to marking.

ASSESSMENT AND DEVELOPMENT OF HOW CHILDREN COMPOSE WRITING

Once a piece of writing has been completed by a child, it is normally only possible to infer the composing processes that went into it. The children themselves may not be able adequately to recall or express how they selected and planned the content and expression. Because of the lack of finite points of reference, a teacher working in the five to 13 age-range will need to use what is known about the pupils' background and writing ability, the circumstances of the writing itself, the original aim, and how it related to other activities, such as visits, discussions or practical work. It is in this area of 'situational assessment' that the primary or middle school teacher can exploit the knowledge and insights which can be gained about children from spending many hours every day with them. The resulting knowledge can be a valuable resource for channelling into a range of possible activities for helping children become aware of how writing can be composed. These activities might include 'facilitative procedures', teacher–pupil conferences and writing with the children.

Recent research in Canada has examined some aspects of children's composing of writing where teachers might effectively intervene by using 'facilitative procedures' (Bereiter and Scardamalia, 1982). These are ways in which the teacher can intervene to ease the burden of composing, without providing any direct help in deciding on the content or form of the final written 'product'. All these aspects of composing are based on features of writing which are distinctly different from communicating by talking and which were reviewed earlier – the lack of turn-taking in written communication, and of the associated inputs from the conversational partner as well as adjustment to the fact that the graphic nature of written language means that it can be planned and reviewed as a 'whole'. The research suggests the use of the following procedures:

● generating pieces of writing by 'prompting';

● searching the children's memories for adequate content by
   brainstorming ideas;
   listing words;

● planning the whole piece, instead of just the parts by
   ending sentences;
   using structures;

● reviewing and revising;

● writing jointly with the children.

Let us examine each of the procedures in turn.

The research reported by Bereiter and Scardamalia outlines how various aspects of the language production system can be developed in ways which might serve various writing goals. Even in paying attention just to these aspects teachers may well be able to 'nullify' certain symptoms of composing problems, by contriving the conditions of writing so as to by-pass the point of difficulty or by carrying out a task for a child.

Generating pieces of writing by prompting

When Bereiter and Scardamalia have experimented with the effects of giving nine- to 11-year-olds 'contentless prompts' to write more on an opinion, the children produced relatively far more 'structural elements' (reasons, examples, elaborations) than when they attempted the same tasks by talking or slow dictation, although they used more words when talking. Rather than seeing such prompts as oppressive, it is reported that the children welcomed them as 'positive aids' in the composing process. Bereiter and Scardamalia suggest that helping children to develop such self-cueing for themselves can be an important stage in early writing development.

Memory searches for content

However, a more fundamental problem for children seems to be finding content, rather than the language to express it. This second aspect of the composing process into which Bereiter and Scardamalia have researched – learning to make an active search for content – partly draws upon the research on the effects of prompting. The latter had provided indications that children had nowhere near exhausted their knowledge on a topic, even though their capacity to write on it had been 'milked dry'. Bereiter and Scardamalia suggest that 'children's main problem with content is in getting access to, and giving order to, the knowledge they have' (Bereiter and Scardamalia, 1982, p. 17).

Two methods were developed of helping nine- to 13-year-old children effectively to gain systematic access to their world knowledge for use in their writing: 'brainstorming' and word listing. 'Brainstorming' (jotting down lists of promising ideas) was only partially successful and perhaps a little surprisingly children reported that they would not be likely to persist with it. A more promising approach was to encourage children to list 'relevant' words as part of their planning. Children adopting this technique doubled their essay length and tripled their use of unusual words. While there was little overall effect on the quality of writing, word listing might well be helpful in the writing of persuasive arguments or where it was important to capture the interest of the reader.

Further experiments looked at the problem of helping children to draw from memory content related to specific goals. A promising method for nine-year-olds was to ask them to write the instructions for a game which they knew well or had recently been taught. Their attempts to write instructions on how to play the game typically involved the main points but overlooked smaller ones. Much more effective instructions were written when the children were shown videotapes of inadequate instructions being used and their unfortunate effects.

Although these experiments were narrowly focused, facilitative procedures for establishing what knowledge is available within the minds of pupils and for encouraging the effective use of such knowledge seem very worthy of further attention in research and teaching. Children may have composing abilities in the junior and middle school years which may need deliberate teaching approaches to bring them properly into use.

Planning the whole piece

The shifting from 'local' to whole-text planning is, like the other aspects of writing development discussed here, related to the differences between the contexts of talking and writing. The elaborate global plan which effective writing often demands is not normally necessary or possible in speech. The responses and reactions of the others in a conversation demand far more adaptability. It is not surprising then that children's writing will frequently lack the 'attention to the whole, and the backward and forward-looking analyses that are the hallmarks of compositional planning' (Bereiter and Scardamalia, 1982, p. 23).

The facilitative procedure which Bereiter and Scardamalia found to be most helpful here was the adoption of 'ending sentences'. These were considerably more helpful to children in developing means-end planning than the use of 'sentence openers' from two or more alternatives which the children were asked to provide for themselves from a pre-established list before beginning each sentence. Children seemed to find it especially helpful to decide in advance upon specific story endings, so that these became part of their initial planning.

A second, less successful, means of generating whole-text planning was the attempt to gain access to and use children's tacit knowledge of the 'language structures' (for example, reasons, descriptions, events) which are found in different kinds of written discourse, such as narrative, argument and the giving of directions. In writing tasks in these three genres, children used more features of each kind of discourse than they could actually name, although there was no evidence that such awareness was consciously used.

Reviewing and revising

Results from experiments have suggested that children can evaluate their first drafts, sentence by sentence (Scardamalia and Bereiter, 1983), but have trouble with improving them and may need considerable outside help in this, probably because they are faced with the highly 'salient' language form of their first draft. Any direct help provided by the teacher can be supplemented from the tacit knowledge gained indirectly from the experience of the children's general reading. This knowledge and experience can be explicitly used in discussion with pupils reading drafts with a 'writer's alertness to technique' (Bereiter and Scardamalia, 1982, p. 44) in relation to problems of composition with which they have struggled.

Graves (1978a; 1983) has put forward a specific teaching strategy to help the revision of writing, the teacher–pupil 'conference'. He shares the priority given by Walker (1974) and Southgate et al. (1981) who have argued for such an approach to be used in both promoting voluntary reading and informally monitoring it. Graves describes in detail how he sees the role of this kind of conference, the different forms it can take and how classroom procedures can be organised to minimise interruptions. Most importantly, though, children need to be given the confidence to conduct a conference on their own terms, genuinely seeking advice from the teacher:

> Teachers can learn to conduct conferences if they start simply. The teacher attends to what children know and helps them to speak about their topics ... For the moment the teacher *puts aside* a concern for mechanics, missing information, and revising to help children get words on paper ... the teacher only attends to what children know and seeks to follow children, helping them all the way to speak about their subjects (Graves, 1983, pp. 104–5).

Writing jointly with the children

A greatly underused approach to helping children to become more aware of the nature and possibilities of the composing process is to write with them. Some kind of joint composing by a teacher and group of children together sharing an agreed task can be illuminating for everyone, including the teacher. Like many adults, teachers may write relatively little of any length in their normal lives. They may not have sufficiently introspected in their own school and college days to be able easily to articulate the way in which the writing of reports, poems, or persuasive arguments can be composed. As was noted earlier in chapter 3, one research study concluded that teachers who do not write themselves in such ways can easily 'underconceptualise and oversimplify the process of composing' (Emig, 1971, p. 98). Joint involvement of this kind may lead to some unexpected findings which may run counter to conventional knowledge – for example it may not be always necessary to write an outline before beginning a draft. This is a view shared by Elbow (1973) who also argues that the best way to understand the nature of writing is regularly to engage in it.

Children can greatly benefit by sharing in the thinking aloud which will go on as they cluster around the blackboard or newsheet. The teacher can act as the secretary or can delegate this role to a pupil, but the vital part of this activity is allowing the children to hear the teacher struggling with them to formulate language to capture the essence of their ideas and 'shaping the ideas at the point of utterance' (Britton, 1972). (I well recall hearing my sixth form English master summing up a discussion on an examination question on Ted Hughes by drafting an introductory paragraph and thinking to myself, 'So this is how it's done!')

The focus of these sessions may well be most easily linked to joint enterprises such as writing a report of a visit, a class experiment, requests, complaints, reactions and so on. Sometimes it may be useful to use one pupil's work as a case study. The recent observational research in primary schools discussed in chapter 2 has shown the value of the kind of discreet sampling which would be useful in selecting a case study. This technique has been also used by Kroll et al. (1980) specifically to monitor children engaged in writing and to speculate about the 'style' of their approaches to it. Occasionally this kind of perceptive observation can be channelled into follow-up work. What the teacher has observed of children's styles of composing might be used as a starting point for 'revisiting' a particular task and situation to see what a group's composing can make of it.

Finally, 'writing jointly with the children' can help the teacher's insights into the nature of children's concepts of writing. It might be possible to integrate the approach of Graves (1975) who asked seven-year-old children what good writers needed to be able to do in order to write well. Children's views on 'getting ideas', 'neatness', 'imagination' can easily be developed in wider discussions and in the continual use of sources of reference whenever the teacher talks with groups or the class on the writing that they do. Children's concepts of writing may influence their writing performance (Kroll et al., 1980).

ASSESSMENT AND DEVELOPMENT OF WHAT CHILDREN HAVE WRITTEN

Approaches to assessing children's writing can follow a whole variety of directions, from the details of spelling through to 'holistic' assessments of the general organisation of what has been written.

'Holistic' assessments of writing (Cooper, 1977) can be based on overall impressions or be scaled in some way. More precise scaling can be applied to certain features, as in the essay scale applied by Martin et al. (1965)

originally for imaginative writing. Here it has been amended slightly to allow it to be applied to writing for a wide range of purposes:

> Has an experience been realistically recreated by language?
> Has the experience been made 'significant' for reader and writer?
> Is the vocabulary precise and appropriate?
> Does the variety of the language used allow a deepening understanding?
> Has the writing been adequately controlled and organised?

Both kinds of approaches have been used by the Assessment of Performance Unit, set up to monitor national standards in several curriculum areas. The analytic assessment for writing of the Unit focuses on:

> content and organisation;
> appropriateness and style (including vocabulary and register);
> grammatical conventions;
> orthographic conventions (including spelling and punctuation).

These kinds of assessment are being made regularly on a range of writing tasks, description, narration, recording, reporting, persuasion, requesting, explaining, planning and editing, in order to build up a data base on children's writing performance on a national basis (Assessment of Performance Unit, 1981).

Some kind of holistic assessment will be important in much of a primary or middle school teacher's work. However, rather than develop analytic scales, many teachers may prefer to use the intimate and emerging professional knowledge of their children and their curriculum framework to approach the assessment and development of children's writing. Any such overall pattern of assessment can be extended by adapting insights from a study of the three principal components of language outlined in chapter 3, the structures of sound-letter relationships, meanings and grammar. The basic pattern can then be related to the overall organisation of the writing in meeting its original aim. When we look at a child's writing, our attention may be given disproportionately to the first of these structures only, for it is the accuracy of the child's spelling which may initially strike us. Because this aspect of writing is seen by so many teachers to be full of so many uncertainties, the following section on spelling is fairly detailed. This is not only to make proper use of some important recent research and publications but also to provide a warning that some established teaching approaches, such as breaking a word into parts and 'sounding it out' in order to spell it, may be ineffective, because of the basic nature of spelling skill.

SPELLING

The dangers of teachers doing little more than 'continually inspecting for flaws' are especially great with spelling, although many will testify to the futility of always reacting to every single spelling error that they see. As

Dunsbee and Ford (1980) remind us, such a pernickety approach is in some ways similar to the long-term effects of continually interrupting someone's speech to correct pronunciation, inflections and hesitations. The speaker might well try to avoid further conversations, or at least become highly inhibited and fail to develop the range of expression that might otherwise have been used. Such inhibitions may develop in children's attitudes to writing in the face of disproportionate concern with uncertain spelling.

A more balanced approach would seem to be to look closely at the factors which are most associated with successful spelling and to teach children in the light of what is known about English spelling patterns. In short, some spelling errors are more acceptable than others. In her authoritative research in the 1960s, Margaret Peters (1970) identified three factors in primary school children which were particularly associated with success in spelling:

> verbal intelligence;
> visual perception of word form;
> carefulness.

The fact that these factors have been found to be more important than auditory skills is especially worthy of note. It is tempting to think of spelling merely as the transcription of speech sounds, but this is an unreal impression, for two important reasons. First, sound–letter relationships are irregular in English, as Berdiansky's (1969) much quoted research indicates. Berdiansky and her colleagues found 211 relationships between letters and sounds (e.g. c*o*t, c*o*at, s*o*rt, m*oo*n) just in a sample of two-syllable words understood by six- to nine-year-old children. Secondly, research suggests that in the development of spelling, vision is our preferred sense. We build up our spelling skill by giving regular visual attention to print. It is significant that if we are not sure of the spelling of a word, we write down our version of it, to see if it 'looks right'. The importance of these factors is such that if children have weaknesses in any two of them, research suggests that they are 'at risk' in being likely to have difficulties in spelling. At the same time, the identification of these factors also indicates that spelling is a different kind of skill from reading, which draws upon a wider range of intellectual and linguistic skills and in which auditory skill is highly important from the reading readiness stage onwards (Thackray and Thackray, 1974).

Like reading, performance in spelling will be partly linked to the influence of children's cultural background, their families' lifestyles, their experience of language and books, and children who have substantial 'strengths' in these areas are likely to 'catch' spelling relatively easily. But, for many children, the systematically planned experiences of the school to help them 'look at words in special ways' will be crucial. Peters' research on a sample of nearly 1,000 children brought her to an unequivocal conclusion:

There is no question that the behaviour of the teacher determines more than any other single factor, whether a child does or does not learn to spell (Peters, 1975, p. 7).

The Bullock Committee seemed to have this finding in mind in one of its firmest recommendations: 'Spelling needs to be taught according to a carefully worked out policy, which should be based upon the needs and purposes of the pupils' own writing not upon lists of words without context' (DES, 1975, p. 528).

It is worth examining the way in which such a policy can involve pupils, teachers, materials and the general context of the work by including basic recommendations such as these:

● sharing an interest in the patterns of language;

● fostering children's spelling strategies and self-concepts;

● using positive diagnosis and teaching;

● critically appraising published teaching materials.

Sharing an interest in the patterns of language

An important part of an effective approach to the growth of spelling ability is the promotion of a shared interest in the patterns of language. There are two principal reasons for this, one being connected with the predictable finding that verbal intelligence is highly related to spelling ability. This confirms the importance of teachers ensuring that they continue to foster children's awareness of words, through talking with them, reading to and with them, sharing jokes and bringing to everyone's attention anything of interest about words and the use of language which crops up at home or in school.

Torbe (1978) outlines several word games which may indirectly help spelling ability and which may be used with groups, or in some cases the whole class. These games include a version of 'Hangman' which takes the letters in order and a 'Look, Cover, Write, Check' game for pairs of children using flashcards. One child shows and says a word from a card for ten seconds and the other images it for a further ten seconds before trying to write it down and then checking it. Such cards can be designed to draw attention to certain letter strings or be part of a concentrated 'hot spot' of spelling for certain subject areas.

The second reason for promoting shared interest in patterns of language is because the nature of the patterns is often not fully appreciated. Although English seems highly irregular because of its irregular sound–letter relationships, these irregularities are part of a wider, more patterned system in which certain combinations of letters are more likely than others and in which other combinations are never found (Albrow, 1972). For example, compare *trondstrab* and *nmouaptbsi*. Both are nonsense words, but only one is plausible in terms of the 'serial probability' of letters in English. Children who are on their way to becoming successful spellers will have a grasp of likely letter combinations through their use of Peters' second factor: visual perception of word form. It is worth repeating one of Peters' oft-quoted findings when she asked nearly 1,000 third year juniors to spell 'saucer'. Less than half managed to spell it correctly. Of the 505 misspellings, there were 209 variations, including many versions which indicated that the children had inadequate knowledge of the nature of English letter strings (saeucng, spienace, sucger). To confirm the differences between spelling and reading, it is salutary to note that in the standardisation of Schonell's *Graded Word Reading Test*, 71 per cent of all eight-year-olds were able to read saucer (DES, 1975, p. 181). Work on language patterns might also include some reference to 'rules' of spelling, for example 'i before e except after c', although few of these rules are entirely reliable.

Anyone who has struggled with the irregularities of English will not be surprised to hear that computers programmed with hundreds of spelling rules have still been unable to spell correctly half the words they were given.

In addition, the relationships between parts of words can be pointed out. Although breaking a word into syllables does not necessarily help in learning its spelling, recognising the bound morphemes of prefixes and suffixes can help, as with dis-appear; dis-appoint.

Fostering children's spelling strategies and self-concepts

It can be short-sighted to become too concerned with what is being 'taught' in schools and insufficiently concerned with what is being 'learned' by the children. Children will 'construct their own realities' and with spelling, these realities will include their own strategy for learning to spell the words that they need to use. Then encouragement from the teacher to look carefully at the patterns of letter groups in words can become part of this strategy, especially if it is linked to some kind of 'rule of thumb'. One of the most useful of these is to

> LOOK at a word,
> COVER the word,
> WRITE the word and
> CHECK with the original word.

As well as being likely to develop a learning strategy which is sensitive to word structure, this simple approach emphasises the use of visual imagery, which the mere copying of words can neglect. More fundamentally, a systematic strategy of this kind can develop a child's self-concept as someone who can make self-guided progress in spelling.

If some words prove to be very troublesome, for example homophones (see chapter 3, page 24), other strategies can be used such as simple mnemonics:

> '*I* belong to th*eir* (not there) team.'
> '*H*ome is *wh*ere (not wear) we go at night.'

These mnemonics will inevitably be idiosyncratic, but can also be fun to devise, and children can help in doing this for words which have regularly proved difficult to learn. Another, less idiosyncratic method for learning difficult words is the multi-sensory approach of Fernald (1943), finger-tracing the shape of a word several times, while saying the word to oneself.

Fostering children's spelling strategies and self-concepts can ease the burden on the teacher's time in supplying words requested by children for use in their writing. One of the main recommendations in the report of the Schools Council project on 'Extending Beginning Reading' (Southgate *et al.*, 1981) is that such a drain on teachers' time should be curtailed by providing:

classroom charts of commonly used, irregular words;
blackboard lists of key content words for specific subject areas;
graded training in the use of appropriate dictionaries or card indexes.

Even more importantly, children can be encouraged to make an attempt at a word to maintain fluency. These attempts can then be checked at the review stage of writing. If the checking is with the teacher, it is likely to be more effective if a personal word book, alphabetically arranged, is compiled and the child shows the attempt as part of the request. The use of such books is probably quite widespread. Less common is the use of a similar book by the teacher. The teacher word book can be used to note down common uncertainties within a class and other points of interest. These can then form the basis of teaching, including classroom charts, lists, other follow-up activities and the games, and the regular classroom talks on the patterns of language mentioned in the last section.

Using positive diagnosis and teaching

This emphasis is very much the obverse of a 'continual inspection for flaws'. A positive approach to spelling entails seeking ways of promoting growth in children's insights and skills. Some children will be 'catching' spelling in an easy, natural way. These children are likely to have strengths in at least two of three factors, namely verbal intelligence, verbal imagery and appreciation of common letter strings, and are also likely to have swift, well-formed handwriting. Where such strengths are leading to steady progress in spelling, regular teaching may not be necessary. As Torbe (1978) suggests, the main task of the teacher with these children is to encourage them to proof-read their writing. This activity can be linked to the 'reviewing and revising' dealt with earlier in this chapter and in chapter 3.

With those children who are having difficulties, however, some kind of structured diagnosis is needed. This can be based on a collection of spelling errors made by a group of children (Torbe, 1978), or by the use of passages of dictation published for this purpose (Peters, 1979). The need for teachers to take note of and adapt their teaching to different types of spelling errors was recognised by the Schools Council publication on record-keeping in primary schools (Clift *et al.*, 1981).

A careful look at the following piece of writing by Wynford (9) will indicate the value of responding to spelling errors in a diagnostic way.

On Munday I boaght a pair
of shoos thay are cald Lofers
I boaght them becos my uthers
wir faling to bits at the frunt
of the soosh thay cust me £5
.80 I got them wear to school
Thay got losels and lether odd
sols thay are lether all rawnd
wen thay wer down I hav mor
lether sols andthe heyels
hav stel lips poot on them

Someone who only inspected it for flaws would find many. However, a more sensitive check shows that there is a clear pattern in Wynford's misspellings. Nearly all of them follow a spelling precedent of some kind.

Munday	– sun
shoos	– boo
thay	– say
wir	– fir
frunt	– grunt
poot	– soot

In a way, these are a 'better' kind of spelling error, for they indicate a degree of auditory perception and considerable awareness of possible relationships between letters and sounds. Wynford's spelling seems to have been adversely influenced by a very narrow phonic approach when being taught to read. His attention needs to be drawn to the visual relationship between words which share letter strings (e.g. should, could, shoulder) whether or not they sound the same.

His ability to remember these shared letter strings in 'his mind's eye' is likely to be improved by regular use of a 'Look, Cover, Write, Check' procedure on words which he needs to use but misspells. Continued encouragement to develop a neater and more fluent handwriting style might help as well. The inconsistencies (wear, wer; shoes, soosh) suggest that he does not proof-read sufficiently, perhaps because of low self-concept as a speller.

Overall, therefore, pieces of writing of this kind are not best received negatively, for their number of errors, but positively, for what these errors suggest about how the pupils' weaknesses may be properly diagnosed and most effectively helped.

Critically appraising published teaching materials

There are nearly fifty published books, sets of books, or kits currently available to teach spelling to children. These materials frequently take a blanket approach to the teaching of spelling regardless of two kinds of 'needs'. One is the need by children for particular words at a particular time. Published spelling lists will inevitably fail to meet this need, although those devised by Arvidson (1963) at least try to anticipate the words that children tend to use in their own writing at certain ages. The second kind of need is related to what children do and do not know. Most published materials do not build in the necessity to carry out some kind of exploration to establish whether or not children can already spell the lists they provide for teaching. Teachers who methodically introduce five words a day to children and test the week's twenty on the Friday can easily overlook this paradox, while also neglecting to help children develop a strategy for learning the words they do need.

These and other crucial questions are raised by a recent cheap and easy to use 'consumers guide', which describes and evaluates all available spelling materials, published by the Centre for the Teaching of Reading at the University of Reading (Peters and Cripps, 1980). On its first page, the guide draws attention to a highly important question which is often undervalued and which takes up the essentially visual aspect of spelling: 'Does the material emphasise groups of words that look the same, however they sound?' In fact only four sets of material actually do this, which suggests that they have not fully incorporated the implications of the research findings of Peters (1970) and Albrow (1972), although the majority do at least avoid inconsistent letter strings and rules which are complex and unreliable.

There are so many of these materials in schools, that it seems churlish not to use some of them if they have already been purchased and they can provide a resource to be adapted and channelled into meeting the needs identified by a teacher's diagnostic work. However, on the basis of what has just been discussed, it is clear that the materials themselves may need to be given some kind of diagnosis to ensure that their most glaring weaknesses are properly countered by the teacher's own work.

VOCABULARY

It is understandable why great emphasis is sometimes given in schools to children using 'new' and 'unusual' words. 'Vivid' vocabulary has been one of the main indices of success for many teachers enthusiastically caught up in the creative writing movement. As was mentioned in chapter 2, the recent HMI survey of first schools reported that in much of the writing observed, the introduction of new words seemed to be the main purpose (DES, 1982a).

The assessment of vocabulary use in this way is beset with difficulties, for reasons that were partly set out in chapter 3. For instance, the use of a word has to be set against the sense in which it is apparently used and also the evidence that the child understands it. What is more, a concern with words or phrases in themselves can detract from an appraisal of the expression of the ideas to which they relate. Douglas Barnes (1969, 1976) has warned of the difficulties faced by children in the early years of secondary education, where teachers may be so concerned that children adopt the technical language of their subject that they may neglect the value of children's more 'everyday' attempts to formulate ideas and understanding. Rosen (1969) takes a similar line of argument, saying that there are dangers of school subject language, used by teachers or in textbooks, looking at children 'across a chasm'. Although children may 'parrot whole stretches of lingo', their understanding of the subjet matter maybe superficial and flimsy.

While accepting these warnings it also has to be recognised that vocabulary growth, however defined, is a necessity throughout the child's school career and for many occupations. In a very thorough and illuminating study of American College 'Basic Writing' students, Shaughnessy (1977, p. 210) concludes that 'vocabulary looms as perhaps the most formidable and discouraging obstacle (in the) struggle for advanced literacy', but later warns (p. 224) that 'For all that a teacher can do . . . there appear to be stubborn (and doubtless individually different) limits to the pace at which words can enter our active vocabularies.'

Therefore any assessment of a child's use of vocabulary in writing must be both cautious and made with due regard for the curriculum framework in which the writing is done, the actual nature of the task and what is known about what kind of 'language experience' the child was able to bring to the task.

With these points in mind, deliberate attempts to develop vocabulary might usefully include the following possibilities, partly based on those put forward by Shaughnessy (1977):

● developing a sensitivity to words;

● learning words;

● indulging in words.

Developing a sensitivity to words

A sensitivity to words in language can be one of the most integral gains in many curriculum experiences and can be generated in individuals by the use of the pupil-teacher conference, which focuses selectively on vocabulary items which might be replaced by more precise ones. This can be especially valuable when children become over-reliant on words like 'nice', 'a lot' and 'got'. The results of simple replacement tasks can also be shared with groups or undertaken by them.

According to recent research, the potential of group discussions as a means of learning envisaged by the Plowden Report (DES, 1967) has not been fulfilled in the primary school years (Galton *et al.*, 1980). There may well be possibilities for rectifying this in the research in Directed Activities Related to Texts (DARTS) at the University of Nottingham (Gardner, 1981), such as group prediction, group sequencing and group cloze texts. Cloze texts, materials which have words systematically deleted and replaced by lines of a standard length, can be prepared on spirit duplicator or other machines to increase children's awareness of both contextual cues and vocabulary alternatives. Of the whole class experiences which may indirectly help vocabulary growth, reading aloud to children will be prominent in the minds of many teachers. Most teachers will have a short-list of books which they suspect will help in this, although any assumption that vocabulary can be 'transplanted' from book to pupil is likely to be misguided. (I remember a teacher once telling me that she was reading *The Wind in the Willows* to a class of eight-year-olds 'for the vocabulary'.) It is more likely that the effect of the teacher regularly reading worthwhile material aloud to a class will be to increase their more general awareness of the richness and possibilities of language.

Two helpful sources are sometimes underused which might be important influences in vocabulary growth, poetry and jokes. Jokes are an obvious way of exploiting homonyms, through homophones and homographs (see chapter 3). A little booklet compiled by the first school children at my own daughter's school contains examples of each.

What did Father Christmas say before he left home?
'I hope it doesn't rain, dear'.

What makes the tower of Pisa lean?
It never eats anything.

Teachers of older junior or middle school children who enjoy sharing such jokes could well launch the production of joke booklets by reading to their class *The Phantom Tollbooth* by Norton Juster, a remarkably contrived, but entertaining story for pun lovers.

Poetry is a second underused source, even though it can be 'the best words in the best order, language used with the greatest possible inclusiveness and power' (DES, 1975, p. 135). In the HMI primary school survey, less than half the observed children turned readily to books for pleasure during the day and at 11, poetry was read by children in only two-fifths of the classes observed, although twice this proportion of classes had poetry read to them.

Learning words

It is likely that for many children reading is a major source of vocabulary growth. Voluntary reading and good use of book collections and libraries have both been associated with reading attainment in research findings (DES, 1975; 1978). There are now clear and flexible guidelines for helping to monitor the match between reader and text by both various formulae and more child-centred methods (Harrison, 1980; Moon, 1982). However, while there has been a 'golden age' of children's fiction, non-fiction books continue to present problems to children, in both their vocabulary and syntax. Perera (1981) identifies three difficulties at the word level in texts: familiar words with unusual meanings (for example 'solution' in science); subject vocabularies (erosion, estuary, deposition); and formal vocabularies (hereafter, specify, locate). Little is known as to how these difficulties are best countered, but glossaries, drawn up by the pupils near the end of a topic or lesson series, can be a useful means of revision and an informative resource for the teacher in work with other children in this subject area.

Indulging in words

Finally, there is much to be said for letting children loose on an informal exploration of their vocabularies and how they can be extended to give full rein to the possibilities of their repertoire. These can be thematic lists with a minimum of structure or linked more formally to different kinds of visual pattern, as in Jimmy's (10) verbal exploration.

Running Water

Gurgling, gushing,
Bouncing over stones,
Jumping, racing, diving,
Eroding, carrying, dumping,
Tug of war, leap frog,
Building, destructing,
Loud, musical,
Dodging, hitting,
Multiplying, decreasing,
Hurry hurry on,
Turning mills,
Splashing, high, low,
Sparkling, gleaming
Rushing, roaring,
Aiming for the sea,

Slow, fast,
Muddy, sandy, clear,
Housing many creatures,
May nifying,
Under bridges,
Towing logs,
Working, Resting,
Fast, slow,
Non stop,
Streaking, sloping,
Damed, breaking dams,
Towing, pushing,
Lifting, falling,
Sorting, mixing,
Sinking, rising,
Destination sea.

SYNTAX AND PUNCTUATION

Sentence length and structure are obvious areas for attempts to develop the range and variation of children's writing. Children's writing may well show an apparent preference for short, simple sentences and indicate the need for general elaboration or variety in style. Or there may be a more complex problem in which there is a variation in sentence structure but the sentences include some non-standard forms which are inappropriate in the school setting.

It is also worth dealing with punctuation in this kind of context, because an important role of punctuation is to help confirm the structural pattern of words in order to clarify the meaning intended.

But like other aspects of language considered here, there are a number of qualifications to be made. As with reactions to spelling or vocabulary which exclusively focus on specific criteria, crude assessments of sentence length or structure can be inappropriate if the overall effectiveness of the writing in achieving a particular aim is forgotten. Take for instance Andrew's (9) account:

```
MY DOG'S DEATH

On Sunday at three o' clock we
heard a squeal and I saw my
dog Whiskey was lying in the
road bleeding. I picked him
up and put him on the grass and
comforted him.  Mum phoned for
the vet in the telephone box.
But the vet was too late. Whiskey
was dead and I leaned over him and
cried and the man said "I am sorry,"
and I said "It does not matter now
he is dead."
```

In passing this to me in a collection for a school magazine, a teacher had written underneath, 'Good for him – he's remedial.' The assumption here would seem to be that the short, bald statements lack the complexity and verbal embellishments sought after in, say, creative writing teaching. As an evocative record of an emotional release through writing, though, it is remarkably successful.

Again with caution in mind, some possible teaching strategies for developing flexibility in the use of syntactical structures and of punctuation can be investigated:

- encouraging writing where new structures are called for;
- diagnosing features of non-standard dialect;
- promoting discussion of syntactic alternatives;
- explaining the need for punctuation and proof-reading.

Encouraging writing where new structures are called for

For syntactical skill to grow, the situation needs to demand it. The popularity of story-writing in schools has probably contributed to the findings that in complex sentences (see chapter 4), adverbial clauses of time are widely used in the writing of eight-year-old children (Harpin, 1976). The lesser-used clauses in the eight to 11 age-range include those of result (so that...), purpose ('so...'), manner (as...) and concession ('although', 'even if'). These kinds of structures are likely to be used more frequently if some of the apparently neglected tasks, such as persuasive writing, were undertaken more frequently. Note here the use of a range of structures by Simon (11), involved in the production of a 'local tourist guide':

Tourists

Abingdon is one of the most beautiful and historic towns in the whole of the Thames Valley. It is for this reason that the visitors come. Some visitors get their first glimpse of the town from the River Thames, which flows swiftly through the town. Others come by road and see the tall spire of St. Helens Church, towering high into the sky. There are other attractions such as the Abbey Meadows, coaching inns, old grey walls and beautiful gardens. Or you can enjoy your favourite sports, whether its bathing, boating, fishing, golf on a fine springy course, bowls, tennis or just lazing in the shade.

> You can stroll far from the crowd or mingle with the merry bustle on market days. There are boating trips to Oxford from Abingdon if you enjoy boating. There is a swimming pool in the Abbey Meadows, and also a non-swimmers pool. Despite some industrialisation, Abingdon retains its character of Saxon times which mingles with the beauty and leisure of the river.

As well as structures within sentences, more attention can be given to the structures between sentences, part of what is often called 'textual cohesion'. Cohesion can be achieved by a variety of means such as intonation (in speech) and by a careful choice of vocabulary:

The boy ran on to the beach. The sand was soft and warm.

Halliday and Hasan (1976) have identified four main kinds of syntactical cohesion:

1 *reference:* John hummed to himself. This helped him to relax.

2 *substitution:* A car came up the road. It was the same one as before.

3 *ellipsis* (omission): He tried to run. He couldn't.

4 *conjunctives:* (i) *additive,* e.g. and, next, also, besides;
(ii) *adversative,* e.g. yet, but, however, though;
(iii) *causal,* e.g. so, therefore, as a result;
(iv) *temporal,* e.g. then, later, next, after that.

For many teachers it would probably be too artificial deliberately to contrive writing tasks for the use of such devices; these can easily become 'dummy-run' exercises. But if writing tasks are encouraged which allow for a framework of aims such as those adopted in this book, then these possibilities for cohesion can be used as a helpful resource for teaching and discussion.

Diagnosing features of non-standard dialect

There are many children whose written syntax can be lively and varied but who use different features from those of standard English. In syntax these features may be of various kinds ('Yesterday he comes up the road'; 'Pick up them shoes'; 'He hasn't got no crayons') and may be accompanied by some features of non-standard vocabulary. This is a particularly complex issue for teachers and is further complicated if non-standard dialect is used by children from ethnic minorities. If such features are a recurrent part of children's writing, they are also likely to be an integral part of not only their speech, but also their parents'. Because of these deeply-rooted factors, any attempt to eradicate a non-standard dialect like West Indian Creole is likely to be unsuccessful. Instead, children will need to be helped to bring an additional dialect, standard English, into their repertoire. As yet, this strategy has apparently not been widely adopted in multiracial schools (DES, 1982b). Teachers are naturally reluctant to be thought of as tacitly encouraging 'poor' language use. Increasingly, however, linguists are publicising the view that non-standard dialects are well-developed systems of language and that differences from a standard form should be used positively as part of the language curriculum.

Such a positive approach to the differences can be founded on a study of the non-standard forms, such as that provided by Edwards (1979) or by White (1972), on West Indian language use. A 'bidialectal' approach to teaching demands a good deal of faith and can even be the subject of criticism by the very groups whom it is most designed to help (see Edwards, 1979, p. 108). An important step towards this approach is openly to channel non-standard forms into writing where familiarity with them can be seen as a strength. This is especially effective in expressive kinds of writing and where dialogue is used, as with Anne's (10) attempt to capture the Jamaican dialect at her family's breakfast time and Yvonne's (11) record of a conversation between her mother and her brother.

Promoting discussion of syntactic alternatives

Cloze procedure has already been mentioned as a possible way of increasing awareness of vocabulary alternatives. In completing such a text which has been 'modified' by deletions, children also have to use the contextual cues provided by the text. A recent detailed book on cloze procedure (Rye, 1982) discusses these and other uses. Current work by Gardner (1981) is exploring cloze procedure in innovative ways including the deletions of phrases, clauses and whole sentences. Provided the text is worth reading and the material is taken from a source within the mainstream curriculum activities of the class, phrase, clause and sentence deletion could prove to be a helpful way of promoting discussion of syntactic alternatives. A second way of promoting this kind of discussion could come from the work on sentence-combining in the United States (e.g. O'Hare, 1973):

At the breakfast table

Today at de breakfast tebal mi mada say to mi get de suga and cereal pan de tebal. And we all set dawn to breakfast. Mi When mi mada say why you put so much suga pan you breakfast, mi hope you yam off every Lickle grain a suga on it. Dhen all of a sudden mi brada nock off all deah milk pan de tebal. Mi mada just Look pan him and say you betta wipe off all dat milk. Dhen mi Papa come dawn deah Stairs and him just Fling him self dawn on he did lan pan mi

Shopping

MUM:- Wane com bwoy com op to de shop fa mi Nu

Wane:- But mi waent to play withd mi fren dem

Mum:- Mi se if you nu do as your tole mi ago find out

Wane:- Okay den but can ni get mi choclate

MUM:- Yes qwan an hurry up because mi have to go out

Wane:- Bye

MUM:- Yes chile qwan boat you buesnis

The old man was walking up the hill.   *As the old man was*
walking up the hill, a
little boy called
A little boy called to the old man.   *to him.*

As Smith (1982, p. 229) acknowledges, this is one of the few forms of 'English exercises' where there is some evidence of an improvement in writing fluency. Shaughnessey (1977, p. 78) suggests that sentence-combining offers the inexperienced writer the nearest equivalent to finger exercises in music. Some teachers will baulk at this kind of disembodied activity, but, by ensuring that the subject matter has a familiar point of reference, the effects of sentence-combining seem worthy of further investigation in classroom work.

Explaining the need for punctuation and proof-reading

The accuracy of punctuation and spelling is frequently adopted as one of the main criteria in assessing writing. This is a misleading pairing in some ways, because whereas the system of spelling is almost entirely 'established', punctuation is more flexible. Well known writers vary in their use of punctuation: Roald Dahl indulges in a remarkable number of exclamation marks; Frank Smith confesses to using the dash far more than many writers; and the poet e e cummings virtually dispenses with punctuation.

It may be more helpful to consider punctuation as a resource which is woven into syntax to help confirm meanings. This link with meaning is important to bear in mind for teaching and can help avoid the familiar problem of children sprinkling a newly-learned symbol indiscriminately throughout their writing. Children will vary enormously in their ability to hold thoughts on 'punctuation plans' within their consciousness along with so many other skills and processes.

It seems that children's awareness of the need for and uses of punctuation will be best modelled on some kind of ordered teaching which fits their ability to handle this extra demand. Harpin (1976) argues that the full-stop is of fundamental importance and can be linked with the tone variations of the question mark and exclamation mark. Children will be 'catching' punctuation awareness from home or their reading, and their growing perceptions can be consolidated by stressing the use of certain punctuation features in what they read, from group or class language-experience newsheets onwards. The use of capital letters for beginning sentences and names is an obvious priority in this. In some ways, the use of commas has a less precise function than these conventions and writers vary somewhat in their use. As their most established function is probably to replace words, such as 'and' in lists which occur in prose, this might be a useful way to introduce them.

From here, it can be shown how commas can help show where a main idea is being modified in some way, as in the sentence which precedes the one you are now reading. Amusing examples can be used to show children how the addition of a comma can indicate fundamental differences in meaning: 'Shoot, Jones!' compared with 'Shoot Jones!'

It is sometimes suggested that some features of punctuation can be best taught by showing their necessity in the act of reading aloud. In this way the links between both pauses (commas, full stops, capital letters) and intonation (questions and exclamations) and punctuation can be demonstrated. This may well be so, but with an important qualification. The value will come from the act of responding to written language, not by listening to speech. Because of the looser, 'chained' syntax of speech (outlined in chapter 3), many of its pauses are less likely to be of a kind indicated by punctuation. Instead, pauses in speech tend to be thinking spaces, used whenever an idea or word has to be formulated or where the listener seems likely to interject.

A more realistic way to develop the use of punctuation is likely to be in encouraging proof-reading. As Smith (1982) notes, such punctuation occurs 'late' in texts, anyway. Thus syntax and punctuation can be 'refined' together, to shape the meaning intended for the audience. Proof-reading can become part of children's revising processes, studied by Graves (1979), in which personal experience and writing for peers seem to be influential. This kind of approach has advantages over any kind of textbook punctuation exercise which may lack the support of a purposeful and meaningful context. Moreover, such purposeful writing can utilise information which is not present in the isolated exercises of a textbook which are, by definition, out of context. It is obviously within a communicative context that other types of punctuation (apostrophes, colons and semi-colons) can be best introduced with upper junior or middle school pupils, as well as continuing attention paid to layout and paragraphing. Here too, the use of the proof-reading skill can be fostered by some kind of draft on which others are invited to comment, as was suggested in chapter 7.

WHEN DEVELOPMENT IS SLOW

When development of children's writing is unusually slow, detailed attention may need to be given to several of these different aspects of the process. As the children grow older, they may also have a mature sense of frustration which can be channelled into some kind of guided systematic self-appraisal. Some interesting possibilities in this area of work have been outlined by Binns (1980).

The core of Binns' work is focused on drafting and redrafting. These procedures are designed on three main assumptions:

1   that children want to go on working on a particular piece of work;
2   that the teacher does not write in corrections;
3   that weaknesses in the flow of ideas and words are exploited by reading over drafts and discussing them.

Among the procedures which Binns has encouraged in children are:

● reading over passages (silently or aloud) to explore the relationship between 'sound, form and meaning' (Halliday, 1975);

● using a double page spread: left hand for notes; right hand for drafts and final version;

● developing a notation system for recording errors and anticipated changes.

The strength of this kind of approach is that the pupil is involved in an essentially active way and, whatever the nature of the weaknesses, is never on the receiving end of the 'continual inspection for flaws' discussed earlier. Furthermore, attention is not just on the products of writing but on the processes, allowing the incorporation of insights gained from recent research in composing, outlined earlier in the chapter. It also allows for a good deal of negotiation between teacher and pupil, in which attention can be directed at mutually agreed aspects of the writing.

The focus of Binns' work is perhaps a little narrow, for he does not mention the importance of context and aim in writing, although he does note the importance of motivation, even though the example of drafting which he includes is a rather stereotyped war story, unconvincingly written in the first person. Drafting and redrafting may be most effective where a clearly identified aim and audience within a realistic context provides even greater support and motivation for the drafting process. Also such approaches to drafting and redrafting may be just as appropriate for children who are making steady development as writers. For these may also gain from a staggered shift from unvarying attention on rapidly written one-off products to greater indulgence in the nature of the production process. The idea of a double page spread for drafting can be widely applied in all kinds and stages of writing, for instance. (In fact, it was used in the writing of this book.)

APPROACHES TO MARKING

The marking of children's writing, adding written notes and comments to it, is a very personal matter and individual styles of approach will inevitably be varied, according to children's performance and needs. Many teachers will have worked out their own 'system', including not necessarily writing anything at all, but talking over the matters which arise, suggesting a redraft or encouraging the children themselves to write in evaluative comments or notes for future reference.

However, wherever writing is 'marked' in any sense of this word, it is important to bear in mind some of the main implications which spring from what has been set out in this chapter. The following suggestions are inevitably speculative but can be used to trigger off further thought and discussion:

- positively adapt the marking approach to the circumstances (including 'conferences' and agreed notation for labelling 'errors');

- if comments are made, ensure that *what* is written receives attention before *how* it is written;

- consider all the contextual factors of written language use;

- record instances of gross errors for future teaching plans.

Rather than deal with each of these in turn, the following diagram represents an attempt to bring these considerations together coherently:

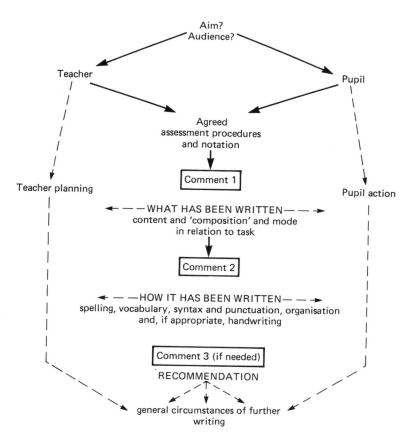

Overall circumstances of the writing

Aim?
Audience?

Teacher

Pupil

Agreed
assessment procedures
and notation

Comment 1

Teacher planning

Pupil action

— — WHAT HAS BEEN WRITTEN — — →
content and 'composition' and mode
in relation to task

Comment 2

← — — HOW IT HAS BEEN WRITTEN — — →
spelling, vocabulary, syntax and punctuation, organisation
and, if appropriate, handwriting

Comment 3 (if needed)

RECOMMENDATION

general circumstances of further
writing

This diagram helps to draw attention to certain points which can be easily overlooked: the possibilities for agreeing the context of the writing and how it is likely to be received; the different aspects on which teachers can focus their attention when assessing writing and commenting upon it; the possible links between what is done at a particular time and future action and planning.

Such points may seem straightforward enough, but it seems likely that many schools still have a long way to go fully to exploit the dynamic relationships between them.

This chapter has attempted to outline various possibilities for helping children to develop the complex network of skills which together contribute to their overall writing performance. These possibilities are inevitably drawn from a wide range of sources, as the general perspective of this book has been. It seems apt, therefore, to draw together a few final thoughts on what has emerged from the analysis undertaken in the writing of this book in a short, final chapter.

10 Final words

A book is many-faceted and each reader will take different things from it. I outlined the various kinds of audience for whom this book is intended in chapter 1. The principal audience is the practising teacher; to be more precise and realistic, the 'thinking teacher', who is continually at pains to evaluate his or her work. With the growth of school-focused in-service activities, the thinking teacher is increasingly likely to be involved in generating activities with colleagues as part of the 'thinking school'. With such school-based activities in mind, it is appropriate to end with some firm recommendations which might serve as a helpful focus for the putting together of a school's written language policy and which might also help to structure the use of this book in that kind of staff development process. The five simple statements below may seem a little obvious, but if the rest of the book has been effectively consulted, their significance may be better appreciated. Perhaps a sense of *deja vu* may greet some of these recommendations, but judging from the evidence surveyed earlier in the book, there can be a gap between what teachers may think they are doing and what they are actually doing when their practice is assessed systematically.

1 CULTIVATE AN INTEREST IN LANGUAGE

Underlying the whole of this book is an assertion of the importance of a professional understanding of the nature and growth of language. It is an understanding which can have far-reaching ramifications. For instance, teachers' reactions to variations in accent and dialect can play a key part in the shaping of attitudes of different social groups towards school. These reactions need to be particularly sensitive and balanced in the multicultural *milieu* of contemporary British society. In addition, teachers' attempts to develop components of children's writing such as spelling or vocabulary are likely to be more effective if based on a well-founded understanding and appreciation of the systematic and patterned features of language outlined in chapter 3. Even more importantly, teachers need to be aware of the ways in which the use of language can foster thinking, especially the fundamental influences of the experience of talking with others. Some of the arguments on this are speculative and at times controversial, but it seems very likely that in many cases a major factor in school performance is the quality of dialogue that a child has with others.

2 CONSIDER THE CONTEXT OF CHILDREN'S WRITING

This recommendation is intended to act as a reminder of the dynamic relationship between what children bring to a writing task, the curriculum arrangements within which it occurs, and the principal dimensions of the writing, its aim, audience, content and mode. Few studies of writing in primary and middle schools have properly taken account of these kinds of dynamic relationship. A few years ago, Connie Rosen's (1973) studies of classroom practice in over 20 local education authorities suggested that the issuing of a title, on which the children immediately began writing, was a widespread practice. Whether or not this is still the case is not clear from the available evidence, but it seems likely that a critical assessment of the kinds of issues highlighted by the 'three-dimensional' diagram in chapter 7 (page 77) would considerably enrich the curriculum planning of many schools, including the ways in which children's written work is received and assessed. There seems little doubt in the minds of HM Inspectors in their most recent report on nine to 13 middle schools that 'In general . . . children need more opportunities to write for a variety of purposes in a range of styles and to write for real or imagined readers other than teachers' (DES, 1983, p. 58).

Related to these thoughts is the need to appraise the classroom conditions in which children write. Chapter 2 outlined the recent findings on pupil behaviour types and how some of the trends might be related to cycles of activity in writing tasks. Perhaps children are encouraged to put pen or pencil to paper for an unrealistic amount of the time and need to be encouraged to give more time to planning and composing, as well as drafting and redrafting. Perhaps they are encouraged to write for unrealistic amounts of the school day without opportunities to engage in other kinds of constructive activity, including purposeful talk. However, because of the need to wrestle with what Vygotsky (1962) called the 'abstract, deliberate activity' of writing, classroom conditions will need to help children in what Lopate (1977) calls 'learning to be alone' in the special, psychological sense which is needed for many of the writing tasks in which they engage.

3 PROVIDE SUPPORT FOR CHILDREN WRITING

Teachers generally provide support for children writing in a good number of ways and many of these are outlined in chapters 6–9. But there are two possibilities which may well be under-exploited. One is to make more of what children write available for other children to read. 'Writing for others' is a well-known slogan which has not been translated into practice as widely as it might have been. The sensitivity of a teacher's support can exploit children's capacities in such directions as small books of poems or stories, illustrated by the children themselves and also read by them on to tapes for a particularly individualised kind of listening and reading activity. The techniques of book production in itself can provide a natural consolidation of such work, techniques set out in a very detailed and practical book by Bennett and Simmons (1978).

Children seem to write in the modes of description and narrative more readily than the modes of classification and evaluation and this may be related to a lack of available models of this latter kind of writing. It is certainly worth asking how much non-fiction is read aloud to children, for it is here that the latter modes tend to be used. My guess is that, compared with the reading of fiction, normally presented in a predominantly narrative mode, children have very little non-fiction read to them. Therefore a second possibility of additional support is to read aloud more non-fiction as well as examples of children's attempts to take on the kind of writing aims which employ classification and evaluation, so much part of references to the world or persuasive arguments (see chapter 8). Such reading aloud might help to provide a broader background of experience and opportunities for teaching and discussion, on which children can indirectly draw in the development of their own writing.

4 PLAN INTERVENTIONS

An understanding of the nature of language, a realistic context and sympathetic support may not be enough. Many children will need carefully planned interventions by teachers to encourage practice and growth in aspects of writing identified by well-founded diagnostic assessment. Chapters 7 and 8 indicated how a framework of writing aims can be used as a backcloth for such appraisal and intervention. Chapter 9 provided many practical ideas for the teaching which can follow. Chapter 6 considered some of the main issues as children are initiated into the early stages of writing, while chapters 4 and 5 sketched out some of the criteria which have been attributed to the succeeding stages and dimensions in later writing development.

Of all these ideas, two in particular seem to me to warrant urgent attention by teachers and researchers: drafting and reviewing. We need to know much more about the ways in which children might be helped to become writers by doing what skilled adults often do: they draft and redraft. The use of word processors may prove to be a help in this.

Similarly when and how children can be effectively helped to review their writing seem very worthy of detailed investigation. Within a credible network of writing aims, reviewing and the proof-reading which goes with it, appear essential skills to encourage in children's approaches to writing. Nevertheless, we know little about what is involved in this. There may be unexpected resistance from psychological and social constraints in the same way that children and students appear generally slow to react to any encouragement to use flexible approaches in reference book use (Neville and Pugh, 1975; Lunzer and Gardner, 1979). There is much to be done to encourage young readers to look on; in the same way young writers have to be encouraged to look back.

5 WRITE YOURSELF, IN FRONT OF THE CHILDREN

A recent report on extending beginning reading recommended that teachers of seven- to nine-year-olds organise regular silent reading lessons, of increasing length (Southgate, 1981). The recommendation is also that teachers read their own books alongside the children to add conviction to the activity. Whatever is gained from this kind of joint enterprise, there probably is as much, if not more, to be gained from teachers writing in front of the children, tailoring the manner in which this is done to the children's abilities and ages.

Silent writing, though, is not sufficient. Far more is likely to be gained from the teacher attempting writing which has something of a challenge in it, a haiku poem, an amusing anecdote, or a polite letter of complaint to a touchy neighbour, with the teacher thinking aloud in front of groups of children as the writing is composed and written on a surface where they can easily follow the words as they appear. This kind of exercise resembles in principle the spoken part of the advanced driving test and could be a revelation for teacher and pupils alike, especially if the children are likely to be involved in comparable challenges in their own work. Writing yourself, in front of the children in this way could provide many insights into how writing is composed, transcribed and reviewed and the complexity of the interrelationships.

There may be something even more to be gained for teachers themselves from such activities. Many adults will probably suffer writing 'blocks' from time to time, with procrastination culminating in a wild dash of writing at the very last moment. Writers who have considered this problem, such as Smith (1982) and Elbow (1973), are agreed on the way to tackle it: keep the pen moving. As Smith (1982, p. 13) puts it, the distinguishing feature about people who overcome writing blocks is that '. . . they write. They live with their uncertainties and difficulties and they write.' Regularly writing with the children could conceivably be part of such a strategy.

THE YOUNG WRITER AS 'AUTHOR'

This book ends as it began, with a young writer. The final extract of writing highlights what children can achieve as authors. Moffett (1979) distinguishes between several definitions of writing: handwriting, transcribing, copying, paragraphing, crafting and 'authoring'. He argues that educators should primarily conceive of writing in the final sense, 'the authentic expression of an individual's own ideas . . . source content not previously abstracted and formulated by others' . . . a 'focused and edited version of inner speech . . .' (Moffett, 1979, p. 278).

Diana's (10) remarkable piece of writing is a memorable example of such 'authoring'. It was written entirely voluntarily, being triggered off by family circumstances which can possibly be inferred from the curious mix of amusement and solemnity which reading the piece may bring to mind. As a piece of writing it stands as a reminder of the writing and the use of writing which can occur in the primary school years if the context is really favourable.

Age

Age is like a jigsaw.
Each person has a jigsaw with 100 pieces in it. Each year one piece is filled in. I am 10 and so a tenth of my jigsaw is done.
Not many people finish their jigsaw. They get bored roundabout the 80th piece.
Those who do finish it get sent a special letter from the Queen and they do another shorter jigsaw.

Most of all, it stands as a testimony to what children are capable of, when they write.

Bibliography

Page references are given in **bold type** at ends of entries.

AJURIAGUERRA, J. DE and AUZIAS, M. (1975) 'Preconditions for the development of writing in the child', in LENNEBERG, E. H. and E. (eds.) *Foundations of Language Development: A Multidisciplinary Approach Vol. 2.* New York: Academic Press. **31, 59**

ALBROW, K. H. (1972) *The English Writing System: Notes towards a Description.* London: Longman for Schools Council. **123, 127**

ALLEN, D. (1980) *English Teaching Since 1965: How much Growth?* London: Heinemann Educational Books. **55**

ANDERSON, R. C. (1977) 'The notion of schemata and the educational enterprise', in ANDERSON, R. C. *et al.* (eds.) *Schooling and the Acquisition of Knowledge.* Hillsdale, New Jersey: Lawrence Erlbaum Associates. **30**

ANDREWS, R. and NOBLE, J. (1982) *From Rough to Best.* London: Ward Lock Educational. **87**

APPLEBEE, A. N. (1978) *The Child's Concept of Story.* Chicago, Illinois: University of Chicago Press. **30, 63, 69**

ARMITSTEAD, P. (1972) *English in the Middle Years.* Oxford: Basil Blackwell. **2, 49**

ARVIDSON, G. L. (1963) *Learning to Spell.* Exeter: Wheaton. **127**

ASHWORTH, E. (1973) *Language in the Junior School.* London: Edward Arnold. **50**

ASSESSMENT OF PERFORMANCE UNIT (1981) *Language Performance in Schools: Primary Survey Report No. 1.* London: HMSO. **121**

BANTOCK, G. (1980), cited in RICHARDS, C. (ed.) *New Directions in Primary Education.* Lewes: The Falmer Press (p. 13). **75**

BARNES, D. *et al.* (1969) *Language, the Learner and the School.* Harmondsworth: Penguin Books. **128**

BARNES, D. (1976) *From Communication to Curriculum.* Harmondsworth: Penguin Books. **128**

BEARD, R. M. *et al.* (1978) *Research into Teaching Methods in Higher Education* (4th edition). University of Surrey: Society for Research into Higher Education. **30**

BENNETT, L. and SIMMONS, J. (1978) *Children Making Books.* London: A. and C. Black. **143**

BENNETT, N. (1976) *Teaching Styles and Pupil Progress.* London: Open Books. **78**

BENNETT, N. *et al.* (1980) *Open Plan Schools.* Windsor: National Foundation for Educational Research (NFER) for Schools Council. **2, 10, 11, 12, 17, 18**

BERDIANSKY, B. *et al.* (1969) 'Spelling-sound relations and primary form-class descriptions for speech-comprehension vocabularies of 6–9-year-olds. South West Regional Laboratory for Educational Research and Development, Technical Report No. 15', cited in SMITH, F. (1978) *Understanding Reading* (2nd edition). New York: Holt, Rinehart and Winston. **122**

BEREITER, C. (1980) 'Development in writing', in GREGG, L. W. and STEINBERG, E. R. (eds.) *Cognitive Processes in Writing.* Hillsdale, New Jersey: Lawrence Erlbaum Associates. **2, 35, 40–1, 42, 57**

BEREITER, C. and SCARDAMALIA, M. (1982) 'From conversation to composition: the role of instruction in a developmental process', in GLASER, R. (ed.) *Advances in Instructional Psychology, Vol. 2.* London: Lawrence Erlbaum Associates. **29, 30, 62, 113, 116–17, 118, 119**

BINNS, R. (1980) 'A technique for developing written language', in CLARK, M. M. and GLYNN, R. (eds.) *Reading and Writing for the Child with Difficulties.* University of Birmingham: Educational Review Occasional Publications No. 8. **137**

BIRD, J. (1982) *Young Teenage Reading Habits* (British National Bibliography Research Report No. 9). London: British Library. **7**

BLACKIE, J. (1963) *Good Enough for the Children?* London: Faber and Faber. **51**

BRIGGS, D. (1970) 'The influence of handwriting on assessment', *Educational Research*, **13**, 1. **69**

BRITTON, J. (1971) 'What's the Use? A schematic account of language functions' in *Educational Review*, **23**, 3, 205–19. Reprinted in CASHDAN, A. and GRUGEON, E. (eds.) (1972) *Language in Education.* London: Routledge and Kegan Paul. **7, 54**

BRITTON, J. (1972) *Language and Learning.* Harmondsworth: Penguin Books (first published by Allen Lane, The Penguin Press, 1970). **59, 120**

BRITTON, J. *et al.* (1975) *The Development of Writing Abilities (11–18).* Basingstoke: Macmillan. **2, 54**

BRITTON, J. *et al.* (1979) 'No, no, Jeanette!', *Language for Learning*, **1**, 1, 23–41. **56**

BROWN, R. (1968) Introduction, in MOFFETT, J. *Teaching the Universe of Discourse.* Boston, Massachusetts: Houghton Mifflin. **26–7**

BROWNJOHN, S. (1980) *Does It Have To Rhyme?* London: Hodder and Stoughton. **98**

BROWNJOHN, S. (1982) *What Rhymes With 'Secret'?* London: Hodder and Stoughton. **98**

BRUNER, J. S. (1960) *The Process of Education.* New York: Vintage Books.

BRUNER, J. S. (1972) *The Relevance of Education.* London: Allen and Unwin. **21**

BURGESS, C. *et al.* (1973) *Understanding Children Writing.* Harmondsworth: Penguin Books. **2, 29**

CLARK, M. M. (1974) *Teaching Left-Handed Children.* London: Hodder and Stoughton. **72**

CLAY, M. M. (1975) *What Did I Write?* Auckland, N.Z.: Heinemann. **66**

CLAY, M. M. (1980) 'Early writing and reading: reciprocal gains', in CLARK, M. M. and GLYNN, T. (eds.) *Reading and Writing for the Child with Difficulties*, University of Birmingham: Educational Review Occasional Publications No. 8. **65**

CLEGG, A. (ed.) (1964) *The Excitement of Writing*. London: Chatto and Windus. **45, 46, 50**

CLIFT, P. *et al.* (1981) *Record Keeping in Primary Schools*. Basingstoke: Macmillan for Schools Council. **125**

COHEN, L. and MANION, L. (1983) *Multicultural Classrooms*. Beckenham: Croom Helm. **76**

COOPER, C. R. (1977) 'Holistic Evaluation of Writing' in COOPER, C. R. and ODELL, L. (eds.) *Evaluating Writing: Describing, Measuring, Judging*. State University of New York at Buffalo, National Council of Teachers of English. **120**

COOPER, C. R. and ODELL, L. (eds.) (1978) *Research on Composing: Points of Departure*. Urbana, Illinois: National Council of Teachers of English. **28**

COSIN, B. *et al.* (eds.) (1971) *School and Society*. London: Routledge and Kegan Paul in association with The Open University Press. **6**

COWIE, H. (ed.) (1984) *The Development of Children's Imaginative Writing*. London: Croom Helm. **63**

CRYSTAL, D. (1976) *Child Language, Learning and Linguistics*. London: Edward Arnold. **22, 23, 25**

CRYSTAL, D., FLETCHER, P. and GARMAN, M. (1976) *The Grammatical Analysis of Language Disability*. London: Edward Arnold. **26**

CUTFORTH, J. A. (1954) *English in the Primary School* (2nd edition). Oxford: Basil Blackwell. **43–4**

DALE, P. S. (1976) *Language Development: Structure and Function* (2nd edition). New York: Holt, Rinehart and Winston. **23**

DEAN, J. (1968) *Reading, Writing and Talking*. London: A. and C. Black. **46**

DEARDEN, R. F. (1971) 'What is the integrated day?', in WALTON, J. (ed.) *The Integrated Day in Theory and Practice*. London: Ward Lock Educational. **76**

DES (1959) *Primary Education*. London: HMSO. **53**

DES (1967) *Children and their Primary Schools* (The Plowden Report). London: HMSO. **53, 129**

DES (1970) 'Primary School English'. *Trends in Education*, 18, 3–9. London: HMSO. **53**

DES (1975) *A Language for Life* (The Bullock Report). London: HMSO. **2, 8, 14, 15, 18, 20, 24, 26, 53, 55, 72, 123, 124, 129, 130**

DES (1978) *Primary Education in England*. London: HMSO. **2, 6, 7, 10, 52, 53, 75, 76, 130**

DES (1982a) *Education 5 to 9: an illustrative survey of 80 first schools in England*. London: HMSO. **2, 10, 23, 52, 128**

DES (1982b) *Bullock Revisited: A discussion paper by HMI*. London: Department of Education and Science. **98, 134**

DES (1983) *9–13 Middle Schools: An illustrative survey*. London: HMSO. **142**

DIXON, J. (1975) *Growth through English* (3rd edition). Oxford: Oxford University Press for the National Association for the Teaching of English (NATE). **6, 54**

DOLAN, T. *et al.* (1979) 'The incidence and context of reading in the classroom', in LUNZER, E. and GARDNER, K. (eds.) *The Effective Use of Reading*. London: Heinemann for Schools Council. **11, 12, 18**

DONALDSON, M. (1978) *Children's Minds*, London and Glasgow: Collins (Fontana). **6**

DONOUGHUE, C. *et al.* (eds.) (1981) *In-Service: the Teacher and the School*. London: Kogan Page in association with The Open University Press. **8**

DOWNING, J. (1969) 'How children think about reading', *Reading Teacher*, 23, 3, 217–30. Reprinted in CHAPMAN, L. J. and CZERNIEWSKA, P. (eds.) *Reading: From Process to Practice*. London: Routledge and Kegan Paul in association with The Open University Press. **59**

DUNSBEE, T. and FORD, T. (1980) *Mark My Words: A study of teachers as correctors of children's writing*. London: Ashton Scholastic in association with Ward Lock Educational. **115, 122**

EDWARDS, V. K. (1979) *The West Indian Language Issue in British Schools: Challenges and Responses*. London: Routledge and Kegan Paul. **26, 134**

ELBOW, P. (1973) *Writing Without Teachers*. New York: Oxford University Press. **29, 42, 120, 144**

ELLIS, A. (1968) *A History of Children's Reading and Literature*. Oxford: Pergamon Press. **7, 120**

EMIG, J. (1971) *The Composing Processes of Twelfth Graders*. Urbana, Illinois: National Council of Teachers of English. **32**

FERNALD, G. M. (1943) *Remedial Techniques in Basic School Subjects*. New York: McGraw-Hill. **125**

FLOWER, L. S. and HAYES, J. R. (1980) 'The dynamics of composing: making plans and juggling constraints', in GREGG, L. W. and STEINBERG, E. R. (eds.) *Cognitive Processes in Writing*. Hillsdale, New Jersey: Lawrence Erlbaum Associates. **28, 29**

FREDERIKSEN, C. H. and DOMINIC, J. F. (eds.) (1981) *Writing: The Nature, Development and Teaching of Written Communication. Vol. 2, Writing: Process, Development and Communication*. London: Lawrence Erlbaum Associates. **30**

GAGG, J. C. (1955) *Teaching Written English*. London: Newnes. **44**

GAHAGAN, D. M. and GAHAGAN, G. A. (1970) *Talk Reform*. London: Routledge and Kegan Paul. **60**

GALTON, M. *et al.* (1980) *Inside the Primary Classroom*. London: Routledge and Kegan Paul. **2, 10, 12, 13, 77, 129**

GALTON, M. and SIMON, B. (eds.) (1980) *Progress and Performance in the Primary Classroom*. London: Routledge and Kegan Paul. **77, 78**

GANNON, P. and CZERNIEWSKA, P. (1980) *Using Linguistics: An Educational Focus*. London: Edward Arnold. **24**

GARDNER, K. (1981) *Directed Reading Activities*. Nottingham: University of

Nottingham School of Education, mimeo. **129, 134**

GIORGI, A. (1976) 'Phenomenology and the foundations of psychology', in ARNOLD, W. J. (ed.) *1975 Nebraska Symposium on Motivation*. Lincoln, Nebraska: University of Nebraska Press. **5**

GRAVES, D. H. (1975) 'An examination of the writing processes of seven-year-old children'. *Research in the Teaching of English*, 9, 227–241. **2, 79, 120**

GRAVES, D. H. (1978a) *Balance the Basics: Let them Write*. New York: Ford Foundation. **119**

GRAVES, D. H. (1978b) 'Handwriting is for writing'. *Language Arts*, 55, 393–399. **59, 71, 72**

GRAVES, D. H. (1979) 'What children show us about revision'. *Language Arts*, 56, 3, 312–319. **137**

GRAVES, D. H. (1983) *Writing: Teachers and Children at Work*. London: Heinemann. **119**

GRAY, J. (1980) 'How good were the tests? (Review of the ORACLE project)'. *The Times Educational Supplement*, 7 November (p. 17). **79**

GREGORY, M. and CARROLL, S. (1978) *Language and Situation: Language Varieties and their Social Contexts*. London: Routledge and Kegan Paul. **34**

GREGSON, J. M. (1973) *English*. London: Macmillan. **48**

HAGGITT, T. W. (1967) *Working With Language*. Oxford: Basil Blackwell and Mott. **47, 48**

HALLIDAY, M. A. K. (1970) 'Language structure and language function', in LYONS, J. (ed.) *New Horizons in Linguistics*. Harmondsworth: Penguin Books. **21**

HALLIDAY, M. A. K. (1975) *Learning How to Mean*. London: Edward Arnold. **24**

HALLIDAY, M. A. K. and HASAN, R. (1976) *Cohesion in English*. Harlow: Longman. **133**

HALSEY, A. H. (1981) *Change in British Society* (2nd edition). Oxford: Oxford University Press. **5**

HARPIN, W. (1976) *The Second 'R': Writing Development in the Junior School*, London: Allen and Unwin. **2, 35, 36, 40, 41, 43, 53, 74, 79, 132, 136**

HARRI-AUGSTEIN, S. et al. (1982) *Reading to Learn*. London: Methuen. **110**

HARRIS, J. and KAY, S. (1981) *Writing Development: Suggestions for a Policy 8–13 years*. Rotherham: Metropolitan Borough of Rotherham Education Committee. **37**

HARRISON, C. (1980) *Readability in the Classroom*. Cambridge: Cambridge University Press. **130**

HAYES, J. R. and FLOWER, L. S. (1980) 'Identifying the organisation of writing processes', in GREGG, L. W. and STEINBERG, E. R. (eds.) *Cognitive Processes in Writing*. Hillsdale, New Jersey: Lawrence Erlbaum Associates. **33**

HENDERSON, E. S. (1979) 'The concept of school-focused in-service education and training'. *British Journal of Teacher Education*, 5, 1, 17–25. **8**

152 CHILDREN'S WRITING IN THE PRIMARY SCHOOL

HOFFMAN, M. (1976) *Reading, Writing and Relevance.* London: Hodder and Stoughton. 110
HOLMES, N. (1967) *The Golden Age for English.* London: Macmillan. 47
HOURD, M. L. and COOPER, G. E. (1959) *Coming into Their Own.* Republished 1971, London: Heinemann. 44, 79
HUTCHCROFT, D. M. R. *et al.* (1981) *Making Language Work.* London: McGraw-Hill. 2, 55, 65, 67
INGHAM, J. (1982) *Books and Reading Development* (2nd edition). London: Heinemann. 98
JAMES, A. and JEFFCOATE, R. (eds.) (1981) *The School in the Multicultural Society.* London: Harper and Row in association with The Open University Press. 76
JONES, A. and MULFORD, J. (eds.) (1971) *Children Using Language.* London: Oxford University Press. 50–1, 54, 55
JOOS, M. (1962) *The Five Clocks.* Indianapolis, Indiana: Indiana University Press. 43
KERRY, T. (1982) *Topic Work in Progress.* Nottingham: University of Nottingham. 75, 76
KING, M. L. and RENTEL, V. (1979) 'Toward a theory of early writing development', *Research in the Teaching of English*, 13, 3, 243–253. 62
KING, P. R. (1979) *Nine Contemporary Poets: a Critical Introduction.* London: Methuen. 31
KINNEAVY, J. L. (1971) *A Theory of Discourse.* Englewood Cliffs, New Jersey: Prentice Hall. 14, 56–7, 90, 110
KOHL, H. (1967) *36 Children.* Harmondsworth: Penguin Books. 42
KRESS, G. (1982) *Learning to Write.* London: Routledge and Kegan Paul. 69
KROLL, B. M., KROLL, D. L. and WELLS, C. G. (1980) 'Researching children's writing development: the children learning to write project'. *Language for Learning*, 2, 53–80. 2, 120
KROLL, B. M. and WELLS, C. G. (eds.) (1983) *Explorations in the Development of Writing.* Chichester: John Wiley. 59
LANE, S. M. and KEMP, M. (1967) *An Approach to Creative Writing in the Primary School.* London: Blackie. 2, 46–7
LANGDON, M. (1961) *Let the Children Write.* London: Longmans, Green. 45
LAWTON, D. (1974) 'Curriculum', in OWEN, R. (ed.) *Middle Years at School.* London: BBC Publications. 8
LEE, L. (1977) *I Can't Stay Long.* Harmondsworth: Penguin Books. 30
LINDSAY, P. H. and NORMAN, D. A. (1972) *An Introduction to Psychology.* New York: Academic Press. 29
LLOYD-JONES, R. (1977) 'Primary trait scoring', in COOPER, C. R. and ODELL, L. (eds.) *Evaluating Writing: Describing, Measuring, Judging.* State University of New York at Buffalo: National Council of Teachers of English. 57
LOPATE, P. (1977), cited in GRUNDLACH, R. A. (1981) 'On the nature and development of children's writing', in FREDERIKSEN, C. H. and DOMINIC,

J. F. (eds.) *Writing: The Nature, Development and Teaching of Written Communication. Vol. 2* (p. 143). **142**

LUNZER, E. and GARDNER, K. (eds.) (1979) *The Effective Use of Reading.* London: Heinemann for Schools Council. **11, 12, 143**

LURIA, A. R. (1959) 'The directive function in speech in development and dissolution', *Word,* **15**, 3, 341–52. Reprinted in OLDFIELD, R. C. and MARSHALL, J. C. (eds.) (1968) *Language,* Harmondsworth: Penguin Books. **21**

LYONS, J. (1970) *Chomsky.* London: Collins (Fontana). **25**

MACKAY, D. and SIMO, J. (1976) *Help Your Child to Read and Write, and More.* Harmondsworth: Penguin Books. **61**

MACKAY, D. *et al.* (1980) *Breakthrough to Literacy, Teachers' Manual* (3rd edition). London: Longman for Schools Council. **22, 60**

MALLETT, M. and NEWSOME, B. (1977) *Talking, Writing and Learning 8–13* (Schools Council Working Paper 59). London: Evans/Methuen for Schools Council. **55**

MARK, J. (1976) *Thunder and Lightnings,* Harmondsworth: Penguin Books (Puffin). **76**

MARSHALL, S. (1974) *Creative Writing.* London: Macmillan. **2, 49, 50**

MARTIN, N. C. *et al.* (1965) *Assessing Compositions.* Glasgow: Blackie. **120**

MARTIN, N. *et al.* (1976) *Writing and Learning Across the Curriculum 11–16.* London: Ward Lock Educational. **2**

MAYBURY, B. (1967) *Creative Writing for Juniors.* London: Batsford. **2, 46**

MERRITT, J. E. (1977) 'Higher order reading skills', in The Open University, *Developing Independence in Reading* (Course PE231, 'Reading Development' Block 2). Milton Keynes: The Open University Press. **110**

MINISTRY OF EDUCATION (1954) *Language: Some Suggestions for Teachers of English and others.* London: HMSO. **53**

MOFFETT, J. (1968) *Teaching the Universe of Discourse.* Boston, Massachusetts: Houghton Mifflin. **35, 37–8, 41, 62**

MOFFETT, J. (1979) 'Integrity in the teaching of writing'. *Phi Delta Kappan,* **61**, 4, 276–279. **144**

MOON, C. (1982) *Individualised Reading: Comparative Lists of Selected Books for Young Readers* (14th edition). Reading: Centre for the Teaching of Reading, University of Reading School of Education. **130**

MULFORD, J. (1969) 'The Primary School', in THOMPSON, D. (ed.) *Directions in the Teaching of English.* London: Cambridge University Press. **52**

MURRAY, D. (1978) 'Internal revision: a process of discovery', in COOPER, C. R. and ODELL, L. (eds.) *Research on Composing: Points of Departure.* Urbana, Illinois: National Council of Teachers of English. **33**

NATE (1969) 'Writing'. *English in Education,* **3**, 3, Autumn. The National Association for the Teaching of English in association with Oxford University Press. **51**

NEVILLE, M. H. and PUGH, A. K. (1975) 'Reading ability and ability to use a book: a study of middle school children'. *Reading,* **9**, 3, 23–31. **143**

ODELL, L. *et al.* (1978) 'Discourse theory: implications for research in composing', in COOPER, C. R. and ODELL, L. *Research on Composing: Points of Departure*. Urbana, Illinois: National Council of Teachers of English. **28, 29, 57**

O'HARE, F. (1973) *Sentence Combining: Improving Student Writing Without Formal Grammar Instruction*. Urbana, Illinois: National Council of Teachers of English. **134**

OLSON, D. R. (1977) 'From utterance to text: the bias of language in speech and writing'. *Harvard Educational Review*, **47**, 3, 257–281. **22**

PALMER, F. R. (1976) *Semantics*. Cambridge: Cambridge University Press.

PEARSON, P. D. and JOHNSON, D. D. (1978) *Teaching Reading Comprehension*. New York: Holt, Rinehart and Winston. **30**

PEEL, M. (1967) *Seeing to the Heart*. London: Chatto and Windus. **48**

PERERA, K. (1981), 'Some language problems in school learning', in MERCER, N. (ed.) *Language in School and Community*. London: Edward Arnold. **130**

PETERS, M. L. (1967) *Spelling: Caught or Taught?* London: Routledge and Kegan Paul. **69**

PETERS, M. L. (1970) *Success in Spelling*. Cambridge: Cambridge Institute of Education. **122, 127**

PETERS, M. L. (1979) *Diagnostic and Remedial Spelling Manual* (revised edition). London: Macmillan. **122–3, 125**

PETERS, M. and CRIPPS, C. (1980) *Appraisal of Current Spelling Materials*. Reading: Centre for the Teaching of Reading, University of Reading School of Education. **127**

PIAGET, J. (1959) *The Language and Thought of the Child* (revised edition). New York: Harcourt Brace and World. **21**

PUFFIN BOOKS (1978) *The Crack-a-Joke Book*. Harmondsworth: Penguin Books. **24**

PUMFREY, P. D. (1976) *Reading: Tests and Assessment Techniques*, London: Hodder and Stoughton (new edition pending). **115**

PYM, D. (1956) *Free Writing*. London: University of London Press Ltd. **44**

RABAN, B. (1982) *Influences on Children's Writing 5–9 Years*. Paper presented at UKRA Conference, Newcastle, July. **59**

RANCE, P. (1968) *Teaching by Topics*. London: Ward Lock Educational. **75**

RICHARDS, C. (ed.) (1980) *Primary Education: Issues for the Eighties*. London: A. and C. Black.

RICHARDS, C. (ed.) (1982) *New Perspectives on Primary Education*. Lewes: The Falmer Press. **75**

ROBERTS, G. R. (1972) *English in Primary Schools*. London: Routledge and Kegan Paul. **48–9**

ROSEN, C. and ROSEN, H. (1973) *The Language of Primary School Children*. Harmondsworth: Penguin Books for Schools Council. **2, 58, 142**

ROSEN, H. (1969), cited in BARNES, D. *et al. Language, the Learner and the School*. Harmondsworth: Penguin Books (p. 12). **128**

RYE, J. (1982) *Cloze Procedure and the Teaching of Reading*. London: Heinemann. **134**

SASSOON, ROSEMARY (1983) *The Practical Guide to Children's Handwriting*. London: Thames and Hudson. 72

SCARDAMALIA, M. (1981) 'How children cope with the cognitive demands of writing', in FREDERIKSEN, C. H. and DOMINIC, J. F. (eds.) *Writing: The Nature, Development and Teaching of Written Communication. Vol. 2*. London: Lawrence Erlbaum Associates. 31

SCARDAMALIA, M. and BEREITER, C. (1983) 'The development of evaluative, diagnostic and remedial capabilities in children's composing', in MART-LEW, M. (ed.) *The Psychology of Written Language*. Chichester: John Wiley. 119

SHAUGHNESSY, M. P. (1977) *Errors and Expectations: A guide for the teacher of basic writing*. New York: Oxford University Press. 32, 69, 128, 136

SHELDON, S. (1982) *A Study of Techniques for Teaching and Testing Reading Comprehension*. Milton Keynes: The Open University Faculty of Educational Studies (M.A. Degree Thesis). 110

SHUY, R. W. (1981) 'Towards a Developmental Theory of Writing', in FREDERIKSEN, C. H. and DOMINIC, J. F. (eds.) *Writing: The Nature, Development and Teaching of Written Communication. Vol. 2*. London: Lawrence Erlbaum Associates. 35, 42

SMITH, F. (1978a) *Understanding Reading* (2nd edition). New York: Holt, Rinehart and Winston. 4

SMITH, F. (1978b) *Reading*. London: Cambridge University Press. 4

SMITH, F. (1982) *Writing and the Writer*. London: Heinemann. 4, 21, 30, 32, 136, 137, 144

SMITH, N. and WILSON, D. (1979) *Modern Linguistics*. Harmondsworth: Penguin Books. 25

SMITH, P. (1977) *Developing Handwriting*. London: Macmillan. 72

SOCKETT, H. (1976) 'Teacher accountability', *Proceedings of the Philosophy of Education of Great Britain*, Vol. X, July, 34–55. Reprinted in FINCH, A. and SCRIMSHAW, P. (eds.) (1980) *Standards, Schooling and Education*. London: Hodder and Stoughton in association with The Open University Press. 4

SOUTHGATE, V. *et al*. (1981) *Extending Beginning Reading*, London: Heinemann for Schools Council. 11, 16, 17, 18, 41, 79, 119, 125, 144

TAYLOR, B. and BRAITHWAITE, P. (1983) *The Good Book Guide to Children's Books*, Harmondsworth: Penguin Books. 98

TAYLOR, J. (1973) *Reading and Writing in the First School*. London: Allen and Unwin. 65

TAYLOR, P. H. and RICHARDS, C. (1979) *An Introduction to Curriculum Studies*. Windsor: NFER. 76

THACKRAY, D. and THACKRAY, L. (1974) *Thackray Reading Readiness Profiles: Manual of Instructions*. London: Hodder and Stoughton. 122

THOMAS, L. F. and HARRI-AUGSTEIN, E. S. (1976) *The Self-Organised Learner and the Printed Word* (Report to the Social Science Research Council). Uxbridge: Brunel University, Centre for the Study of Human Learning. 110

THOMAS, N. (1980) 'The Primary Curriculum: survey findings and implications', in RICHARDS, C. (ed.) *Primary Education: Issues for the Eighties.* London: A. and C. Black. **9, 75**

THORNTON, G. (1980) *Teaching Writing.* London: Edward Arnold. **27–8**

TORBE, M. (1978) *Teaching Spelling* (2nd edition). London: Ward Lock Educational. **123, 125**

TOUGH, J. (1976) *Listening to Children Talking.* London: Ward Lock Educational. **115**

TOUGH, J. (1977) *The Development of Meaning.* London: Allen and Unwin. **21, 60**

TRUDGILL, P. (1975) *Accent, Dialect and the School.* London: Edward Arnold. **23**

TUCKER, B. (1973) *Teaching English in the Middle Years.* London: Ward Lock Educational. **49**

VINCENT, D. and CRESSWELL, M. (1976) *Reading Tests in the Classroom,* Slough: NFER. **115**

VYGOTSKY, L. S. (1962) *Thought and Language.* Cambridge, Massachusetts: MIT Press. **142**

WALKER, C. (1974) *Reading Development and Extension,* London: Ward Lock Educational. **119**

WELLS, G. (1977) 'Language use and educational success; an empirical response to Joan Tough's "The Development of Meaning (1977)"'. *Research in Education,* 18, 9–34. **21**

WELLS, G. (1981a) *Language and Learning: Some Findings and Suggestions from the Bristol Study of Language and Development at Home and at School.* Bristol: University of Bristol, Centre for the Study of Language and Communication, mimeo. **27, 59, 61**

WELLS, G. (1981b) *Learning through Interaction.* Cambridge: Cambridge University Press. **60**

WEST SUSSEX COUNTY COUNCIL (1976) *Children and Language.* Basingstoke: Globe Education. **54**

WHITE, J. *et al.* (1972) *Concept Seven-Nine.* E. J. Arnold for Schools Council. **134**

WHITEHEAD, F. (1976) 'The Present State of English Teaching: 1, Stunting the Growth'. *Use of English,* 28, 1, 11–17.

WHITEHEAD, F. *et al.* (1977) *Children and their Books.* Basingstoke: Macmillan. **7**

WHITEHEAD, F. (1978) 'What's the use, indeed?' *Use of English,* 29, 2, 15–22. **55**

WILKINSON, A. *et al.* (1980) *Assessing Language Development.* Oxford: Oxford University Press. **35, 38, 39, 40, 41, 57, 113**

WILLIAMS, A. (1976) *Reading and the Consumer.* London: Hodder and Stoughton. **110**

WILLIAMS, J. T. (1977) *Learning to Write, or Writing to Learn?* Windsor: NFER. **55**

YARDLEY, A. (1970) *Exploration and Language.* London: Evans. **48**

Subject Index